Criminal Justice
Recent Scholarship

Edited by
Marilyn McShane and Frank P. Williams III

A Series from LFB Scholarly

Delinquency among African American Youth
Parental Attachment, Socioeconomic Status, and Peer Relationships

Steven B. Carswell

LFB Scholarly Publishing LLC
New York 2007

Copyright © 2007 by LFB Scholarly Publishing LLC

Library of Congress Cataloging-in-Publication Data

Carswell, Steven B., 1967-
  Delinquency among African American youth : parental attachment,
socioeconomic status, and peer relationships / Steven B. Carswell.
    p. cm. -- (Criminal justice : recent scholarship)
  Includes bibliographical references and index.
  ISBN 1-59332-195-3 (alk. paper)
  1. African American juvenile delinquents. 2. Juvenile delinquency--
United States. I. Title.
  HV9104.C34 2007
  364.36089'96073--dc22

2006102800

ISBN-10 1593321953
ISBN-13 9781593321956

Printed on acid-free 250-year-life paper.

Manufactured in the United States of America.

~Dedication~

This book is dedicated to my late grandfather, Dr. Odess Edward Hicks, who obtained his Doctorate in Education from Columbia University in 1958. Although he passed away many years ago, the values and beliefs that he instilled in me when I was a child have had a profound impact on shaping the person that I am today. Through the acceptance of his guiding belief in the power of education to overcome racial, social, and economic disadvantage and the knowledge of his own personal achievements, I was able to surmount the many obstacles and challenges that I have faced throughout my life. Without knowing, he was my shining light, the beacon of hope that served as the embodiment of what I could accomplish if I only set my mind, body, and spirit to the task. I will always miss him and forever cherish the time that we spent together, the memories that remain, and the many lessons of life that he taught me.

TABLE OF CONTENTS

LIST OF TABLES

LIST OF FIGURES

~Acknowledgements~

The completion of this book would not have been possible without the generous assistance of numerous individuals who either contributed directly to this work or to my life in a variety of different ways. First, I would like to thank Drs. Kinuthia Macharia, Gloria Young, and Kevin O'Grady for their guidance and support in completing this work. I would also like to extend an additional note of appreciation to Dr. Kevin O'Grady who gave generously of his time and provided much needed advice, review, assistance, and encouragement. In addition, I would like to thank Dr. Thomas Hanlon for the countless hours of advice, guidance, feedback, and support that he has provided to me over the many years that we have worked together. Many thanks also to Ms. Diana Caldwell, Ms. Betsy Simon, and Mr. Jason Callaman who were always available to offer words of encouragement, provide meaningful advice, or to lend a friendly ear whenever I needed to talk. Moreover, thanks are due to the late Dr. Robert Battjes and Mr. Patrick Bogan who never wavered in their belief in my abilities and consistently provided support for my individual research endeavors. I would also like to thank Ms. Pattarapan "Amy" Pothong and Ms. Melissa Harris for their hard work, tireless efforts, and the dedication they displayed in helping me complete this work. Special thanks also go out to the members of my family including my Mother Carolyn, Father Peyton, Sister Lisa, Brother Billy, Aunt Marian, Uncle Saul, late Grandmother Murlenun, and Cousins Kevin, Sybil, and Camille for the love, and invaluable support they have provided me throughout my life. Finally, I would like to thank my wife, Melissa, for her steadfast love, support, and encouragement. She is my best friend and confidant, the person that I turn to when I am happy or sad, and regardless of the challenge or circumstance, she has always believed in me and my abilities.

CHAPTER 1

Introduction

This study evaluates the viability of four conceptual models in explaining the relationships among parental attachment, family socioeconomic status, deviant peer relationships and youth participation in risk behaviors and delinquency among urban African American middle school students. According to Hirschi's social control theory (1969), one of the most widely utilized theories to explain adolescent deviant behavior (Jensen & Rojek, 1992; Kempf, 1993; Lanier & Henry, 1998) and the underlying conceptual framework for the present investigation, delinquency occurs as a result of a lack of bonding between adolescents and society. In the course of development, as posited by Hirschi (1969), attachments and/or bonds are ordinarily formed between youth and conventional others including parents, peers, and teachers with the degree of attachment between parent and child being of particular importance in the later development of delinquency. As such, youth who maintain strong parental attachments are sensitive to the opinions and expectations of their parents and, as a result, are less likely to participate in risk behaviors and delinquent acts. However, if the bonds between parent and child are weak, the extent and frequency of youth participation in such activities becomes progressively greater (Hirschi, 1969).

In addition, there is a growing body of evidence that suggests that family socioeconomic status and deviant peer relationships are important considerations with respect to understanding youth participation in risk behaviors and delinquency (Bellair & Roscigno, 2000; Fergusson, Swain-

Campbell, & Horwood, 2004; Haynie & Osgood, 2005; Leventhal & Brooks-Gunn, 2000; Pardini, Loeber, & Stouthamer-Loeber, 2005; Wright, Caspi, Moffitt, Miech, & Silva, 1999; Weerman & Smeenk, 2005). Empirical research has found that higher family socioeconomic status is related to decreased youth participation in risk behaviors and delinquency, while lower family socioeconomic status is related to increased youth participation in risk behaviors and delinquency (Bellair & Roscigno, 2000; Dodge, Pettit, & Bates, 1994; Fergusson, Swain-Campbell, & Horwood, 2004; Heimer, 1997; LeBlanc, 1992; Sampson & Laub, 1995; Wadsworth, 2000). Moreover, research regarding youth involvement in deviant peer relationships has consistently suggested that such associations are positively related to an endorsement of permissive peer attitudes and deviant peer group norms, thus, increasing the likelihood that youth will participate in risk behaviors and delinquency (Chung & Steinberg, 2006; Elliott, Huizinga, & Ageton, 1985; Heinze, Toro, & Urberg, 2004; Pardini, Loeber, & Stouthamer-Loeber, 2005; Shaw & McKay, 1931; Stormshak, Comeau, & Shepard, 2004; Warr, 2002, 2005; Weerman & Smeenk, 2005). Finally, Patterson et al. (2000) found that deviant peer relationships are an essential feature in the progression of youth deviance and an increased manifestation of multiple forms, or types, of deviant behaviors.

Youth participation in risk behaviors and delinquency are both serious problems in the United States (Farrington, Loeber, Yin, & Anderson, 2002; Miller, Brehm, & Whitehouse, 1998; Smith & Stern, 1997; Stormshak, Comeau, & Shepard, 2004; Thornton, Craft, Dahlberg, Lynch, & Baer, 2000; Weaver & Prelow, 2005). Over the past several decades, empirical research has consistently demonstrated that the early involvement of youth in risk behaviors and delinquency places them in jeopardy of progressing along deviant pathways that, if left unchecked, are likely to continue into adulthood and have life-long detrimental consequences for their health and well-being (Barnes & Welte, 1986; Gottfredson, 2001; Grunbaum et al., 2002; Ingoldsby & Shaw, 2002; Jessor, 1998; Jessor & Jessor, 1977; Newcomb, Maddahian, & Bentler, 1986). Particularly for a significant number of African American youth who live in socially and economically disadvantaged urban communities, are represented among the chronically poor, and are disproportionately exposed to stressful life conditions, initiation and continuation of such problematic behaviors may lead to early school failure, illicit drug use, violent behavior, and the occurrence of premature death (Duncan & Yeung, 1995; Grant et al., 2000; Huston, McLoyd, & Coll, 1994; Jessor, 1993; McLeod & Shanahan, 1993).

For purposes of this investigation, risk behaviors are defined as those acts that have been found to increase the likelihood of youth participation in deviant activities, which may have both negative personal and social consequences (Kandel, Davies, & Krause, 1986; Kirby & Fraser, 1997; Hawkins, Catalano, & Miller, 1992; Hawkins, Catalano, Kosterman, Abbott, & Hill, 1999). Such activities would include school performance problems (low attendance, low grades, and grade repeat); school conduct problems (disruptive classroom activities, suspensions, and expulsions); use of alcohol, tobacco and other drugs (ATODs); and early initiation and involvement in risky sexual activity (nature and extent of activity). On the other hand, delinquency would include those acts committed by individuals under the age of eighteen, which violate the law or the norms of a society (Siegel & Senna, 1991). These acts would include crimes of violence, crimes against property or person, status offenses, that is, those acts considered to be illegal because a child is underage or that violate parental authority, such as running away from home, truancy from school, and curfew violations (Chesney-Lind, 1997; Gavazzi, Yarcheck, & Lim, 2005; Matherne & Thomas, 2001; Siegel & Senna, 1991; Smith & Stern, 1997) and illicit drug possession and/or distribution.

In the United States, the percentage of adolescents participating in risk behaviors and delinquency continues to rise, while the age at which they become involved in such activities continues to fall (Matherne & Thomas, 2001; Smith & Stern, 1997; Stevens & Griffin, 2001). As such, the early identification of the antecedents or precursors that predict youth involvement in such problematic activities has been a major public health objective in the United States for many years (Brounstein, Zweig, & Gardner, 2001a, 2001b; Farrington et al., 2002; Miller et al., 1998; Smith & Stern, 1997; Thornton et al., 2000).

Goals of the Study

The present study utilizes a cross-sectional design and a structural equation modeling statistical approach to evaluate the viability of four models in explaining the relationships among parental attachment, family socioeconomic status, deviant peer relationships and youth involvement in risk behaviors and delinquency. Each of the four hypothetical models has different implications for both theory and prevention research. A prominent feature of all these models is an assessment of the extent to which socioeconomic status may be indirectly related to youth involvement in risk behaviors and delinquency through the mediating variable of parental attachment, an assessment of the extent to which parental attachment impacts on youth involvement in such activities, further clarification regarding the extent to which deviant peer relationships impact on youth involvement in risk behaviors and delinquency, and an examination of African American family relations with respect to family attachment and how such attachments impact on youth involvement in risk behaviors and delinquency, as these are particularly understudied areas of scientific inquiry. Hopefully, this study will contribute to the growing body of knowledge concerning the role that risk and protective factors play in the development of deviant behaviors among youth. In addition, the findings from this study may assist in the design, development, and/or enhancement of preventive interventions aimed at reducing such problem behaviors among youth in general and African American youth living in socially and economically disadvantaged urban communities, in particular.

CHAPTER 2

Mediators of Deviant Behavior

As a result of the dramatic increase in the involvement of youth in deviant behaviors during the past decade, recent research has attempted to identify those risk factors that negatively affect the development of youth (Ingoldsby & Shaw, 2002; Matherne & Thomas, 2001; Reese, 2001; Stormshak, Comeau, & Shepard, 2004). Much of this research has focused on the family (Smith & Stern, 1997) and youth involvement in deviant peer relationships (Haynie & Osgood, 2005; Pardini, Loeber, & Stouthamer-Loeber, 2005; Warr, 2005; Weerman & Smeenk, 2005) with recent work also refocusing on the role of family socioeconomic status and its relationship to youth deviance (Bellair & Roscigno, 2000; Ferguson, Swain-Campbell, & Horwood, 2004; Heimer, 1997; Leventhal & Brooks-Gunn, 2000).

Parental Attachment

Much of the research regarding the risk factors that are related to youth participation in risk behaviors and delinquency has focused on the family and its role in early childhood socialization. Both behavioral scientists and practitioners tend to agree that parents are primarily responsible for instilling and reinforcing within children the values and appropriate behaviors necessary for them to interact with and behave like others in society (Fowles & Kochanska, 2000; Kochanska & Murray, 2000; McNeil, 1969; Schaefer & Lamm, 1998; Shreeber, Hops, & Davis, 2001; Tolan, Cromwell, & Brusswell, 1986). However, if the socialization of the child by the parent is not adequate or appropriate the likelihood increases that children will deal inappropriately with the obstacles and challenges they face within their social and physical environments (Hastings et al., 2000; Hirschi, 1969; Laible & Thompson, 2002; Quay, 1987; Sullivan & Wilson, 1995). Considerable empirical evidence has supported the belief in the primacy of parents as key socializing agents and a frontline defense against delinquency (LaGrange & White, 1985; Parker & Benson, 2004; Siegel & Senna, 1991; Simons, Simons, & Wallace, 2004; Smith & Stern, 1997) as the links between youth parental relationships and delinquency have long been established (Coughlin & Vuchinich, 1996; Glueck & Glueck, 1950, 1968; Herrenkohl et al., 2000; Quay, 1987; Sullivan & Wilson, 1995; Tolan et al., 1986).

Among those family factors that have been found to have the strongest influence on youth involvement in risk behaviors and delinquency are those that relate to parental attachment, that is, the degree of closeness, warmth, respect, and affection shared between parent and child (Akers, 1997; Hirschi, 1969; Simons, Simons, & Wallace, 2004; Wright & Cullen, 2001).   Such close interpersonal relationships between parent and child have been found to provide cohesion and stability within the family, allow for active parental involvement in the lives of children, and enable parents to become acutely attuned to their child's physical, developmental, and social needs as they grow older (Stern & Smith, 1995).   Moreover, youth who maintain such close relationships with their parents have been found to be more accepting of their parents beliefs regarding appropriate behavioral patterns (Arbona & Power, 2003; Quay, 1987; Stern & Smith, 1995) as without such affective bonds, research strongly suggests that youth are at greater risk of becoming involved in risk behaviors and delinquency (Arbona & Power, 2003; Barber & Rollins, 1990; Cernkovich & Giordano, 1987; Hirschi, 1969; Kostelecky, 2005; Maccoby & Martin; 1983; Nye, 1958; Parker & Benson, 2004; Simons, Simons, & Wallace, 2004).

Hirschi's social control theory (1969) has been used as the theoretical framework in much of the research that has explored the relationship between parental attachment and youth delinquency because of its focus on child and parent attachments (Kempf, 1993). According to Hirschi (1969), parental attachment is a "central variable" in social control theory and in examining youth delinquency as a long history of research, including his own, has consistently demonstrated that youth who maintain strong bonds with their parents are less prone to delinquency, as they desire to be viewed positively by them. Moreover, youth may also avoid engaging in such activities out of fear of hurting their parents through their actions and/or because they are concerned about jeopardizing established relationships with them (Thaxton & Agnew, 2004). In addition, Hirschi also posits that even among youth whose parents themselves are deviant, those youth who are attached to such parents are less likely to be deviant (Hirschi, 1969). According to Hirschi, this occurs because these parents instill within their children the importance of adhering to the norms, values, and beliefs practiced by members of mainstream society even if they themselves, at times, deviate from such practices (Hirschi, 1969). However, youth who are less attached to their parents may not be as concerned about their opinions and expectations and, thus, be less inclined to adhere to social norms and values (Hirschi, 1969). Moreover, according to Hirschi (1969), as individuals become increasingly more deviant, their participation in pro-social behaviors and activities may also decrease, resulting in an increase in the frequency and severity of the delinquent acts in which they do participate. Finally, as a result of these adverse circumstances, the nature of their relationships with other members of society may also change, as they are more likely to maintain associations with peers whose bonds to society are also weak, increasing the likelihood that their participation in delinquent activities will become progressively greater (Hirschi, 1969).

Over the past 30 years, Hirschi's social control theory (1969) has been widely used and empirically validated, becoming one of the preeminent theoretical approaches in explaining youth participation in deviant activities (Greenberg, 1999; Jensen & Rojek, 1992; Kempf, 1993; Lanier & Henry, 1998; Siegal & Senna, 1991). Hirschi conducted an evaluation of social control theory based on self-report data obtained from a sample of over 4,000 White and Black male youth (Hirschi, 1969). The results of this evaluation, with respect to the element of parental attachment, suggested that regardless of race or social class, those youth who were more attached to their parents were less likely to report engaging in delinquency than youth who were less attached to their parents (Hirschi, 1969).

As previously indicated, an impressive body of empirical research supports Hirschi's basic contention that an *absence* of parental attachment, and/or bonding, between parent and child is a factor in *freeing* youth for involvement in delinquent activities (Jensen & Rojek, 1992; Kempf, 1993; Lanier & Henry, 1998). In short, this research suggests that youth who are strongly attached to their parents appear to internalize parental beliefs, values, and normative behavioral practices and avoid becoming involved in delinquent activities because they are concerned about hurting them through their actions and/or jeopardizing established relationships with them (Canter, 1982; Hindelang, 1973; Rankin & Kern, 1994; Thaxton & Agnew, 2004; Wells & Rankin, 1988; Wiatrowski, Griswold, & Roberts, 1981). As such, these youth are less likely to become involved in delinquent activities (Arbona & Power, 2003; Barber & Rollins, 1990; Buist, Dekovic, Meeus, & van Aken, 2004; Cernkovich & Giordano, 1987; Maccoby & Martin, 1983; Nye, 1958). Moreover, youth who maintain close attachments with their parents have also been found to be less likely to associate with deviant peers (Kandel & Andrews, 1987; Warr, 1993b, 2005) or to become involved in specific types of delinquent activities, including illicit drug use (Guo, Hill, Hawkins, Catalano, & Abbott, 2002; Kearns & Rosenthal, 2001; Kostelecky, 2005).

Family Socioeconomic Status

Generally defined as a combination of parental education, parental occupation, and family income, socioeconomic status is a concept comprised of two important aspects, one concerned with resources, such as education, income, and wealth, and the other with social status or rank, such as one's social class (Bradley & Corwyn, 2002; Krieger, Williams, & Moss, 1997; McCarthy et al., 2000). Within social science and more specifically in delinquency research, few relationships have been studied more comprehensively than the possible association between family socioeconomic status and youth delinquency (Fergusson, Swain-Campbell, & Horwood, 2004; Heimer, 1997; Leventhal & Brooks-Gunn, 2000; Weiss, 1987; Wright et al., 1999). However, over the past 50+ years, empirical research results regarding the relationship between family socioeconomic status and youth delinquency have been inconsistent, inconclusive, and contradictory (Farrington, 1987; McNulty & Bellair, 2003; Siegel & Senna, 1991; Tittle & Meier, 1990, 1991; Tittle, Villemez, & Smith, 1978; Wadsworth, 2000), as much of this work has attempted to draw *direct* links between family socioeconomic status and youth delinquency (McNulty & Bellair, 2003; Siegel & Senna, 1991; Wadsworth, 2000; Wright et al., 1999). Considered to be the definitive review of this research, Tittle et al. (1978) conducted a meta-analytic review of thirty-five official data and self-report studies that investigated the relationship between family socioeconomic status and youth delinquency and determined that there was inconsistent evidence of direct links between the two at the individual level (Jensen & Thompson, 1990; Siegel & Senna, 1991; Tittle & Meier, 1990; Wadsworth, 2000). Moreover, a subsequent meta-analysis by Tittle and Meier (1990, 1991) again found no consistent support for direct links at the individual level, revealing either weak or nonexistent relationships between socioeconomic status and delinquency, results that were similar in nature to other research findings (Heimer, 1997; Wright et al., 1999). However, sociologists and criminologists have consistently found support for the existence of such a relationship at the aggregate level in view of the fact that research has shown that most juvenile crime occurs in poor, densely populated urban neighborhoods in which residents have few opportunities for social mobility (Blau & Blau, 1982; Box, 1987; Crutchfield, 1989; Ingoldsby & Shaw, 2002; Massey & Denton, 1993; Messner & Golden, 1992; Parker, 1989; Patterson, 1982; Wadsworth, 2000).

As a result of the discrepant findings regarding individual and aggregate level relationships between family socioeconomic status and youth delinquency and because many prominent theories of crime and delinquency are based on the existence of such a relationship at the individual level, theoretical and empirical work over the past two decades has focused on those circumstances in which family socioeconomic status and youth delinquency are strongly correlated at the individual level (Dunaway, Cullen, Burton, & Evans, 2000; Hagan, 1992; Tittle & Meier, 1990, 1991; Wright et al., 1999). Within stratification research, one area of scientific inquiry that examines this issue more closely and that bears directly on the present work investigates the relationship between family socioeconomic status, parental attachment, and their indirect link to delinquency (Fergusson, Swain-Campbell, & Horwood, 2004; Heimer, 1997; Wadsworth, 2000; Wright et al., 1999).

Social stratification theory provides support for investigations regarding family socioeconomic status, parental attachment, and delinquency as this research indicates that socioeconomic status may impact family relationships, including the extent to which parent and child bond, indirectly influencing whether or not youth participate in delinquent activities (Bellair & Roscigno, 2000; Capaldi & Patterson, 1994; Dodge, Pettit, & Bates, 1994; Fergusson, Swain-Campbell, & Horwood, 2004; Heimer, 1997; LeBlanc, 1992; Leventhal & Brooks-Gunn, 2000; Sampson & Laub, 1995; Wadsworth, 2000). As hypothesized by Bellair and Roscigno (2000), this research generally suggests that family socioeconomic status may be related to parental attachment and indirectly to delinquency in the following four ways: First, as family income decreases, parents' emotional distress levels may increase, undermining their ability to bond with their child and maintain close relationships. Second, decreased family income may make it more difficult for parents to provide for their child's material needs, causing some adolescents to lose respect for their parents' opinions, values, and beliefs, potentially inhibiting their acceptance and the subsequent internalization of conventional norms and values. Third, these weakened family bonds and intra-family conflicts may ultimately lead to family instability, as the demands of family life increase for parents due to depressed monetary resources. Fourth, low family income may increase the incidence of family disruptions or conflictual marital relations. Thus, according to Bellair and Roscigno (2000) and other advocates of similar hypotheses, as a consequence of weak parental attachment and family instability resulting from low family socioeconomic status, youth may be less inclined to adhere to their parents' convictions regarding social norms and values and instead participate in deviant behaviors that have more immediate economic and social rewards. Moreover, Capaldi and Patterson (1994) also argue that a lack of economic and social resources and stressful life circumstances may undermine effective family management, which, in turn, may lead to less disciplining and monitoring of youth behavior and correspondingly a greater influence of deviant peer associations and youth delinquency.

As predicted, Bellair and Roscigno (2000) found that family socioeconomic status was positively related to parental attachment and indirectly related to youth involvement in risk behaviors and delinquency. Most noteworthy to this investigation was the finding that low family socioeconomic status appeared to be a factor in both the weakening of parental attachment and the involvement of youth in fighting and drug use during their teen years. Both Dodge et al., (1994) and Fergusson et al., (2004) also found that children from low socioeconomic status families, as compared to children from high socioeconomic families, had increased family adversity, including lower parental attachment; increased attentional and conduct problems; increased school problems (e.g., truancy, suspensions, and low academic achievement); and increased affiliations with delinquent peers who were substance users. Similarly, LeBlanc (1992) found that low family socioeconomic status increased levels of family dysfunction and conflictual marital relations resulting in higher rates of youth delinquency. As such, according to LeBlanc (1992), problematic family relations exacerbated by low family socioeconomic status creates a chain of events that lead to progressively higher rates of youth delinquency as

> ...conflictual marital relations and a tenuous bond will be conducive to inefficient or inappropriate constraints, which, in turn, encourage rebellion against the family and juvenile delinquency during early adolescence and, at the same time, alter by retrospection the bond between the adolescent and the parents and marital relations. Over time, the structural and environmental conditions will be maintained or worsen, the bond will be further impaired, the constraints will be less acceptable and less appropriate for the adolescent age, and offending will continue during late adolescence. This process will prepare the grounds for adult criminality, which will flourish especially if the bond was weak and if delinquency was high during late adolescence (LeBlanc, 1992, p. 351).

Although these initial research findings indicate that a family's socioeconomic status appears to be positively related to parental attachment and indirectly (although inversely) related to youth involvement in risk behaviors and delinquency, conclusions must be tempered because the research evidence is still relatively sparse (Bellair & Roscigno, 2000; Dodge, Pettit, & Bates, 1994; Fergusson, Swain-Campbell, & Horwood, 2004; LeBlanc, 1992; Sampson & Laub, 1995). Moreover, the research that has been conducted has primarily focused on the existence of such relationships among predominately White samples of the population with limited research having been focused on African American family relations and youth friendship patterns, which are both particularly understudied areas of scientific inquiry (Bell-Scott, 1990; Borduin, Pruitt, & Henggeler, 2001; Giordano & Cernkovich, 1993; Kenny, Gallagher, Alvarez-Salvat, & Silsby, 2002; Rodney, Tachia & Rodney, 1999; Weber, Miracle, & Skehan, 1995).

Deviant Peer Relationships

Adolescence is a period of transition for many young people, as it is a time when youth seek and are encouraged to find their place in life through the establishment of their own unique identities, while simultaneously attempting to maintain close relations with family members (Fortenberry, 1998; Laible, Carlo, & Rafaelli, 2000; Miller, 1989; Stoiber & Good, 1998). During their quest for self-identification, many youth may find it easier to relate to their peers, who are similar to themselves in age, life experiences, and perspectives, than their parents (Brown, 2004; Giordano & Cernkovich, 1993; Pardini, Loeber, & Stouthamer-Loeber, 2005; Reyes, Gillock, Kobus, & Sanchez, 2000; Youniss & Smollar, 1985). Moreover, as these relationships grow and mature, the importance and mutual influence of these close associations on youth decisions and their behavior practices may also increase (Giordano & Cernkovich, 1993; Haynie, Silver, & Treasdale, 2006; Kandel, 1978).

Over the years, considerable research and empirical evidence has supported this view, delineating the prominent role that peer relations have on the normal development of adolescents and indicating the extent to which such associations increase or decrease the likelihood of youth involvement in risk behaviors and delinquency (Brown, Eicher, & Petrie, 1986; Chung & Steinberg, 2006; Giordano & Cernkovich, 1993; Dishion, Andrews, & Crosby, 1995a; Dishion, Capaldi, Spracklen, & Li, 1995b; Pardini, Loeber, & Stouthamer-Loeber, 2005; Rankin & Quane, 2002; Stanton et al., 2002; Weaver & Prelow, 2005; Weerman & Smeenk, 2005). This research strongly suggests that youth who associate or become intimately involved in deviant peer relationships are themselves likely to become deviant as the endorsement of deviant peer group norms and their connectedness to the group strongly influences youth involvement in substance abuse (Borden, 2001; Dishion et al., 1995a, 1995b; Elliott et al., 1985, 1989; Fergusson, Lynskey, & Horwood, 1996; Heinze, Toro, & Urberg, 2004; Nurco, Balter, & Kinlock, 1994; Nurco, Hanlon, O'Grady, & Kinlock, 1997a, 1997b; Rosenblum et al., 2005; Stanton et al., 2002; Yanovitzky, 2005); risky sexual behavior (Beier, Rosenfeld, Spitalny, Zansky, & Bontemp, 2000; Doljanac & Zimmerman, 1998; Kirby, 2001; Stanton et al., 1996; Stanton et al., 2002); and serious delinquency (Boyer et al., 2000; Chung & Steinberg, 2006; Greenberg, 1999; Haynie & Osgood, 2005; Henry, 2001). Furthermore, these findings clearly demonstrate the strong tendency of adolescents to commit deviant acts in the company of other like-minded youth (Haynie, 2001; Ingoldsby & Shaw, 2002; Kandel, 1978;

Matsueda & Anderson, 1998; Warr 2002, 2005; Weerman & Smeenk, 2005; Yanovitzky, 2005). Although researchers have found positive associations between youth involvement in deviant peer relationships and their subsequent participation in risk behaviors and delinquency, whether such relationships actually cause these behaviors is still an open question (Guo et al., 2002; Ingoldsby & Shaw, 2002).

However, in studies comparing non-deviant and deviant youth, strong parental attachments have been found to be a prominent protective factor in deterring youth participation in deviant peer relationships and associated deviant acts (Dunst & Trivette, 1994; Hawkins et al., 1992; Howard, Cross, Li, & Huang, 1999; Rutter 1987, 1993; Stanton et al., 2002; Warr 1993b, 2005).

Urban African American Youth

During the past thirty years, researchers have documented the high rates of poverty, unemployment, crime, substance abuse, and other indicators of social disorganization that are becoming increasingly concentrated in America's cities (Jargowsky, 1997; Massey & Denton, 1993; Leventhal & Brooks-Gunn, 2000; O'Donnell, Schwab-Stone, & Muyeed, 2002; Skogan, 1990; Wilson, 1987, 1996). African American youth living in socially and economically isolated urban communities are exposed to a wide variety and increasing number of serious social and environmental risk factors that may severely undermine their life chances (Gallay & Flanagan, 2000; Grant et al., 2000; Kenny, Gallagher, Alvarez-Salvat, & Silsby, 2002; Kasarda, 1992; Rosenblum et al., 2005; Sullivan & Farrell, 1999; Tolan, Gorman-Smith, & Henry, 2003). The emergence and perpetuation of many of these risk factors is directly attributable to, and symptomatic of, the decline in legitimate employment opportunities and the spread of concentrated poverty that has occurred in urban communities since the 1970s and 1980s (Larson, 1988; Jargowsky, 1997; Johnson, Williams, Dei, & Sanabria, 1990; Mouw, 2000; Rankin & Quane, 2002; Wilson, 1987, 1996). Research has indicated that urban joblessness and concentrated poverty spawn a multiplicity of concomitant and interrelated social problems as a lack of available resources leads to increased rates of crime and social disorganization which may increase the likelihood of youth involvement in risk behaviors and delinquency (Brooks-Gunn, Duncan, & Aber, 1997; Leventhal & Brooks-Gunn, 2000; Mouw, 2000; Myers & Taylor, 1998). In spite of progress in identifying risk and protective factors associated with the emergence of deviant behaviors among youth in general, more specific research is needed to identify those factors related to the involvement of urban African American youth in risk behaviors and delinquency, as many of these youth are exposed to serious social and environmental risk factors. Moreover, the involvement of African American youth in deviant behaviors is a particularly serious social concern in the United States, as their involvement in such activities can have both negative individual and social consequences (for further elaboration of this issue see **African American Youth at Risk**, below).

Gender Considerations

Research suggests that consideration of gender differences is fundamental to an understanding of the involvement of youth in risk behaviors and delinquency (Chesney-Lind, 1986, 1997; Daly, 1994; Nichols, Graber, Brooks-Gunn, & Botvin, 2006;

Piquero, Gover, MacDonald, & Piquero, 2005; Rhodes & Fischer, 1993; Sarigiani, Ryan, & Peterson, 1999; Steffensmeier, Schwartz, Zhong, Ackerman, 2005). This research indicates that although adolescent males and females participate in many of the same types of deviant behaviors (Chesney-Lind, 1997; Chesney-Lind & Shelden, 1992; Hartjen & Priyadarsini, 2003; Johnston et al., 2001; Moffitt, Caspi, Rutter, & Silva, 2001; Piquero, Gover, MacDonald, & Piquero, 2005; Wallace Jr., et al., 2003), males are more frequently involved and typically participate in a greater variety of deviant behaviors than females and are more likely to engage in property crimes, substance use, and aggressive or violent behaviors than are females (Agnew, 2001; Barnow, Lucht, & Freyberger, 2005; Chesney-Lind & Shelden, 1992; Herrenkohl, et al., 2000; Loeber & Stouthamer-Loeber, 1998; Piquero, Gover, MacDonald, & Piquero, 2005; Smetana, Crean, & Daddis, 2002). Although, with respect to involvement in aggressive behaviors, recent research has reported high rates of aggression among urban African American females (Blitsten, Murray, Lytle, Birnbaum, & Perry, 2005; Clubb et al., 2001), with one study finding that among sixth and seventh graders, females exhibited greater increases in aggressive behavior than males (Nichols, Graber, Brooks-Gunn, & Botvin, 2006). In general, however, research suggests that females are more likely than males to participate in minor crimes or status offenses including larceny theft, running away from home, truancy, incorrigibility, and milder forms of physical threats or violence (Chesney-Lind, 1986, 1989, 1997, 2002; Chesney-Lind & Shelden, 1992; Morash, 1986; Naffine, 1989; Rhodes & Fischer, 1993; Sondheimer, 2001; Steffensmeier & Schwartz, 2002). Moreover, as posited by Sarigiani et al

(1999) this body of research further suggests that males and females differ in terms of the deviance-related risk and protective factors to which they are exposed within their social and physical environments. This differential exposure not only impacts the underlying motivations for involvement in deviant behaviors but also is an important predictor concerning the specific types and combinations of risk behaviors and delinquent activities in which they are likely to participate (Blake et al., 2001; Chapple, McQuillan, & Berdahl, 2004; Sarigiani et al., 1999; Stevens & Griffin, 2001). Inasmuch as gender differences among males and females with respect to their participation in deviant activities are not clearly understood and as such differences among African American youth as a distinct group, in particular, have not been clearly delineated (Juon, Doherty, & Ensminger, 2006), further investigations of the differential factors associated with the participation of African American males and females in deviant behaviors are clearly warranted.

Outcomes

An extensive research literature supports the importance of both risk and protective factors in influencing an adolescent's decision to avoid or engage in risk behaviors and delinquency (Losel & Bliesener, 1994; Garmezy, 1991; Masten, Best, & Garmezy, 1990; Rutter, 1990). Risk factors are variables that place youth at increased jeopardy of participating in risk behaviors while protective factors aid in preventing youth involvement in such problematic activities by enhancing internal strengths and fostering resilience, enabling adolescents to better cope with adversity (Davis, 1999; Hawkins et al., 1992; Masten & Coatsworth, 1998; Mrazek & Haggerty, 1994; Newcomb et al., 1986; O'Donnell et al.,

2002). It is clear from this research that exposure to an increasing number of risk factors during one's formative years increases the likelihood of youth involvement in risk behaviors and delinquency during adolescence and young adulthood (Bry & Krinsley, 1990; Huizinga & Jakob-Chien, 1998; Masten & Coatsworth, 1998; Newcomb & Felix-Ortiz, 1992; Rankin & Quane, 2002; Rutter, 1980).

Risk Behaviors

Adolescence is a tumultuous period during which many young people undergo physical, psychological, and social changes that prepare them for independence and adulthood (Fortenberry, 1998; LaGrange & White, 1985; Stoiber & Good, 1998). It is also during this period that many youth may begin to participate in risk behaviors, which can have both negative individual and social consequences. Considerable evidence suggests that youth involvement in such activities is related to a variety of serious social, mental, and physical health problems that may place them at high risk for adverse consequences throughout their lifetimes (Dembo et al., 1991; Dryfoos, 1991; Elliott, Huizinga, & Menard, 1989; Sutton, Cowen, Crean, & Wyman, 1999). Furthermore, youth who engage in such problematic activities at an early age generally continue along a stable, predictable path that over time leads to the commission of increasingly serious delinquent acts (Elliott, 1994; Ingoldsby & Shaw, 2002; Loeber, Green, Lahey, Christ, & Frick, 1992; Loeber et al., 1993; Loeber & Hay, 1997; Tremblay, Phil, Vitaro, & Dobkin, 1994).

Empirical research throughout the years suggests that the following types of risk behaviors are either directly or indirectly related to the extent to which youth are attached to their parents.

School Performance and Conduct Problems

Research indicates that youth who fail to develop and maintain strong bonds with their family and who do not feel connected to their school display higher rates of school performance and conduct problems, aggressive and/or violent behavior, substance use, involvement in risky sexual activities, deviant peer associations, and risk behaviors (Dornbusch, Erickson, Laird, & Wong, 2001; Hawkins, et al., 1992, 1999; Mancini & Huebner, 2004; Resnick et al., 1997; Rutter, 1978; Somers & Gizzi, 2001). The negative outcomes associated with the early emergence of school-related problem behaviors has particularly severe consequences for African American students, as compared to White youth, with research finding that African American students are suspended from school more frequently and for longer periods of time (Bennett & Harris, 1982; Reed, 1988; Shaw & Braden, 1990, Voelkl, Welte, & Wieczorek, 1999), and if they drop out of school they are more likely to become involved in delinquent acts at much higher rates (Voelkl et al., 1999). Moreover, African American youth who exhibit early school performance and conduct problems, including school dropout, may severely limit their life chances (Wilson, 1987, 1996), as involvement in such activities may have direct negative consequences on the social and economic opportunities afforded to them, increasing their odds of being unemployed, having significantly lower earnings if employed, and being at greater risk for involvement in delinquency and other criminal activities as they grow older (LeBlanc, 1992; Voelkl et al., 1999).

Alcohol, Tobacco, and Other Drug (ATOD) Use

Studies indicate that poor parental attachments are an especially powerful predictor of adolescent ATOD use (Elliott et al., 1985, 1989; Fergusson et al., 1996; Liska & Reed, 1985; Nurco et al., 1994, 1997a, 1997b) as an absence of parental attachment and/or bonding contributes indirectly to youth involvement in these activities by *freeing* youth for involvement in deviant peer associations and delinquency (Elliott et al., 1985, 1989; Matseuda, 1982; Patterson, Capaldi & Bank, 1989a; Patterson, DeBaryshe, & Ramsey, 1989b). However, results of studies regarding the role of parental attachment with respect to youth behavior when their parents engage in ATOD use are mixed with Jensen and Brownfield (1983) finding that youth attached to drug using parents were neither more or less likely to use drugs themselves while Conger (1976) found that youth deviance *was* related to the level of deviance exhibited by the parent. On the other hand, Dembo et al. (1986) found that low to moderate parental drug use was related to *lower* youth drug use but unrelated if parental drug use was "high," while Bauman et al. (1990) found that youth attached to parents who smoked were themselves more likely to smoke, and finally Sieving et al. (2000) found no support for the hypothesis that a lack of closeness between parent and child influenced the early initiation of alcohol use, although underage alcohol use was influenced by a failure of parent norms to discourage such behavior. Sadly, however, it is a common finding that the early initiation of, and frequent involvement in ATOD use among adolescents is predictive of future involvement in adult deviant behaviors and the consequent occurrence of serious life-long health and adjustment problems (Kandel,

Davies, & Karuse, 1986; OJJDP, 2000; Tomori, Zalar, Plesnicar, Ziherl, & Stergar, 2001; US DHHS, 2001). As such, youth who continue to participate in these activities into adulthood are often economically marginal and at high risk for unemployment (Larson, 1988; Williams & Kornblum, 1985); homelessness (Johnson et al., 1990); and homicide and assault resulting from years of involvement in illicit drug procurement and trafficking (Black & Ricardo, 1994; Li, Stanton, Feigelman, Black & Romer, 1994). Finally, the occurrence of any one or another of these problems among early ATOD users is likely to impair their subsequent functioning as parents, thus increasing the probability that their offspring will also encounter similar situations and circumstances (Goldstein, Hunt, Des Jarlais, & Deren, 1987; Herjanic, Barredo, Herjanic, & Tomelleri, 1979; Johnson et al., 1990; Sowder & Burt, 1980).

Early Initiation and Involvement in Risky Sexual Activities

Since the 1980s, research has shown that youth, especially urban African American youth, are engaging in sexual intercourse at much younger ages than previously reported, with studies indicating first sexual activity occurring between the ages of 13 to 14 and, in many instances, as early as 10 to 11 years of age (Barone et al., 1996; O'Donnell, O'Donnell, & Stueve, 2001; Resnick & Blum, 1994; Stanton et al., 1996). This trend of early engagement in sexual activity is particularly disturbing given research findings indicating that such behavior is associated with multiple problem behaviors, including lower academic performance, gang involvement, emotional distress, suicide, and increased risk of sexually transmitted diseases (STDs), including human immunodeficiency virus (HIV) infection (DiClemente et al.,

2002; Jessor & Jessor, 1975; Resnick & Blum, 1994). The problems associated with adolescent involvement in risky sexual activities are even more troubling for African American youth, who reside in urban communities with high rates of STDs and HIV infection, because of the increased likelihood of their involvement with someone who is HIV-positive (Millstein & Moscicki, 1995; O'Donnell et al., 2001). Moreover, youth who participate in risky sexual activities, including unprotected intercourse, are at greater risk for unwanted pregnancy and single-parenthood, circumstances that may severely limit their ability to complete high school and obtain gainful employment, thus, increasing their odds for long-term poverty and reliance on welfare support (Orr et al., 1991; Stoiber, 1997).

Greater attachment to family has been found to be associated with delays in sexual initiation, less frequent sexual activity, fewer sexual partners, and a greater likelihood of engaging in protective sex among youth (Kirby, 2001), while family conflict has been associated with involvement in health compromising behaviors, including early sexual involvement, particularly among urban African American youth (McBride, Paikoff, & Holmbeck, 2003).

Delinquency

Youth participation in risk behaviors at an early age is particularly troubling considering that one of the most consistent findings in the literature is the strong association between the age of onset and the extent of later delinquent activity (Chaiken & Chaiken, 1982, 1990; Gottfredson, 1987; Loeber & LeBlanc, 1990; Vega, Zimmerman, Warheit, Apospori, & Gil, 1993). This research suggests that the earlier the onset the greater the variety, frequency, persistence, and severity of youth involvement in a host of delinquent activities including crimes of violence, crimes against property or person, status offenses, and illicit drug possession and/or distribution that may continue into adulthood (Anglin & Speckart, 1986, 1988; Centers & Weist, 1998; Elliott el al., 1989; Gavazzi, Yarcheck, & Lim, 2005; Grunbaum et al., 2002; Shaffer, Nurco, & Kinlock, 1984; Siegel & Senna, 1991; Smith & Stern, 1997; Speckart & Anglin, 1986). As summarized by Matherne and Thomas (2001), delinquency is a serious social concern in America as

> It is estimated that in the United States, 1,234 youths run away from home and 2,255 teenagers drop out of school each day. Every five minutes a youth is arrested for some type of violent crime, and every two hours a child is killed by a gun (Edelman, 1995). Taken together, the increase in the number and severity of such delinquent acts and their overwhelming costs for society validates the notion that delinquency has become a prominent national issue (Matherne & Thomas, 2001, p. 655).

Crimes of Violence

As highlighted in the Surgeon General's Report on Youth Violence (US DHHS, 2001), violence among youth is a serious public health problem in America. According to this report, during the decade between 1983 and 1993, the number of youth arrested for serious violent offenses increased by 70%, with homicide rates nearly tripling over this same time period. Snyder (2005) reported that in 2003 alone, 2.2 million youth were arrested, with 15% of them charged with violent crimes. Moreover, violence-related injuries often claim the lives of thousands of young people each year, with homicides being the second-leading cause of death for Americans ages 15-24 and the leading cause of death among African American youth within that same age group (Thornton et al., 2000).

Exposure to violence has become seemingly commonplace in the lives of many urban African American youth (Cooley-Quille, Boyd, Frantz, & Walsh, 2001; O'Donnell et al., 2002; Osofsky, Wewers, Hann, & Fick, 1993; Perez-Smith, Albus, & Weist, 2001; Self-Brown, LeBlanc, & Kelley, 2004; Stewart & Simons, 2006), with over 90% of sixth-grade students in one self-report study indicating that they had heard guns being shot, had viewed people being beaten-up, or had seen the police arrest people in their neighborhoods (Farrell & Bruce, 1997). Such exposure to violence-related activities has been found to be associated with a number of negative outcomes for children and adolescents, including depression, anxiety, and aggressive and/or violent behavior (Daane, 2003; DuRant, Cadenhead, Pendergrast, Slavens, & Linder, 1994; Loeber & LeBlanc, 1990; Martinez & Richters, 1993; Schwab-Stone et al., 1995; Self-Brown, LeBlanc, & Kelley, 2004; Sutton et al., 1999), and if such behavior is initiated during adolescence, it is likely to continue into adulthood (Loeber & LeBlanc, 1990; Sutton et al., 1999).

Crimes Against Property or Person

Empirical research has consistently demonstrated that youth involved in delinquent activities, including crimes against property or person, are vulnerable to the development of deviant lifestyles and the consequent occurrence of serious life-long health and adjustment problems (Jainchill, Hawke, & Messina, 2005; Juon, Eoherty, & Ensminger, 2006; Landsheer & Dijkum, 2005). In general, this research indicates that youth participation in such activities is rarely limited to involvement in one area of deviance but instead tends to encompass multiple areas of deviant or criminal behavior (Crowley & Riggs, 1995; Jainchill, Hawke, & Messina, 2005; Juon, Eoherty, & Ensminger, 2006). For example, in a study by Jainchill, Hawke, & Messina (2005) involving 250 adolescent males and females admitted to a therapeutic community treatment program for substance use, the researchers found extensive youth involvement in multiple criminal activities prior to treatment admission, including drug sales, violent crimes, and property crimes. Such findings are consistent across the literature and have been termed by some researchers as a *general deviance syndrome* (Donovan & Jessor, 1985; Jessor, Donovan, & Costa, 1991; Jessor & Jessor, 1977; McGee & Newcomb, 1992), although one recent study found only modest support for such a designation (Willoughby, Chalmers, Busseri, 2004).

Status Offenses

Youth who engage in status offenses, that is, those acts considered to be illegal because a child is underage or that violate parental authority, account for approximately 14% of juvenile court caseloads (Sickmund, 2000). Although few empirical studies have focused on potential differences between status offenders and youth involved in more serious deviant behaviors (Gavazzi, Yarcheck, & Lim, 2005), available research suggests that the early involvement of youth in such problematic activities increases the likelihood of future offending (Landsheer & Dijkum, 2005; Maxon & Klein, 1997; Riley, Greif, Caplan, & MacAulay, 2004).

Illicit Drug Possession and/or Distribution

Youth growing up in America's urban communities frequently witness illegal activities, including high rates of drug possession and drug distribution (Black & Ricardo, 1994; Centers & Weist, 1998; Okundaye, 2004). The substantial increase in social and environmental problems that have occurred in these areas since 1970 (Jargowski & Bane, 1991; Johnson et al., 1990), coupled with a dwindling employment base for residents of these communities, has led to fewer legitimate occupational opportunities for urban youth who live in these communities (Peterson & Harrell, 1992; Wilson, 1987, 1996). Moreover, government budget cuts as a result of increasing concern by politicians and certain citizen groups over tax increases have reduced community resources and, thereby, exacerbated these serious social problems, creating even greater obstacles to promoting positive behavior. With few available options for social mobility, many youth growing up in these communities become involved in illegal activities, such as drug possession and drug distribution, and in the attendant violence that characterizes such activities (Bell & Jenkins, 1993; Black & Ricardo, 1994; Fagan, 1993; Garbarino et al., 1991; Okundaye, 2004). Despite the growing number of youth involved in such activities, few empirical studies addressing this problem have been conducted (Centers & Weist, 1998). However, one study, conducted by Li & Feigleman (1994), found that in Baltimore City 30% of boys and 40% of girls, between the ages of 9-15 who lived in or near public housing, reported that friends or family members sold or delivered drugs. Available research indicates that youth involved in drug distribution are susceptible to a range of problems including juvenile arrest, substance abuse, and academic failure and dropout (Centers, 1998).

African American Youth at Risk

The involvement of African American youth in risk behaviors and delinquent activities is a serious problem in American society inasmuch as they are more likely than White youth to drop out of school, to be involved in aggressive and violent acts, and to be victims of violent crime (Fraser, Galinsky, & Richman, 1999; Richman & Bowen, 1997; Myers & Taylor, 1998). African Americans are also overrepresented among those adolescents serving time in juvenile detention centers and adult prisons, in morbidity and mortality statistics, and in reports documenting academic underachievement (CDC, 2000; NCES, 2000; NCHS, 2000; Paschall, Ringwalt, & Flewelling, 2003; Snyder & Sickmund, 1999). For example, although African American youth comprised only 15% of the U.S. adolescent population in 1997, they represented 41% of those delinquent youth who were sent to juvenile detention centers and 52% of those youth who were sent to adult criminal court (Paschall, Ringwalt, & Flewelling, 2003; Synder & Sickmund, 1999). In 1998, African American youth accounted for 47% of all adolescent homicide victims between 15-19 years of age, with violence-related mortalities being the leading cause of death among African American youth between 15-24 years of age (Paschall et al., 2003; NCHS, 2000; Thornton et al., 2000). In 2003, even though African American youth accounted for only 16% of the juvenile population, they were overrepresented among those juveniles arrested for involvement in violent crimes (45%) and property crimes (28%), as compared to White youth who accounted for 78% of the juvenile population and were arrested for 53% of violent crimes and 69% of property crimes (Snyder, 2005). High rates of disruptive and violent behavior on school grounds and in the classroom have also been reported for African American youth (CDC, 2000), which have been found to be related to a number of adverse consequences including poor relationships with peers and teachers, high rates of school disciplinary action, and low levels of academic achievement (Gibbs et al., 1988; NCES, 2000; Paschall et al., 2003; Taylor, 1991).

African American youth who live in socially and economically disadvantaged urban environments, in particular, are at high risk for a wide variety of serious educational, social, and physical health problems as they are disproportionately exposed to substandard and overcrowded school environments, illicit drug procurement, distribution, and use, community violence, and high rates of STDs and HIV infection (Black & Ricardo, 1994; Children's Defense Fund, 1995, 2002; Kozol, 1991; Millstein & Moscicki, 1995; Myers & Taylor, 1998; O'Donnell et al., 2001). Research clearly indicates that African American youth living under such conditions are at a disproportionately higher risk for negative personal and social outcomes than are more affluent African American and White youth (Children's Defense Fund, 1995, 2002; Kenny, Gallagher, Alvarez-Salvat, & Silsby, 2002; Myers & Taylor, 1998; Rosenblum et al., 2005). However, the underlying etiological factors associated with the involvement of such youth in risk behaviors and delinquent activities, specifically those factors relating to risk and protection, parent and child relationships, and youth friendship patterns, remain particularly understudied areas of scientific inquiry (Bell-Scott, 1990; Borduin et al., 2001; Epstein, Botvin, Baker, & Diaz, 1999; Fraser, Galinsky, & Richman, 1999; Giordano & Cernkovich, 1993; Kenny, Gallagher, Alvarez-Salvat, & Silsby, 2002; Rodney, Tachia & Rodney, 1999; McKenry, Everett, Ramseur, & Carter, 1989; Paschall et al., 2003; Weber et al., 1995). It is important to ascertain the nature of those etiological factors associated with the development of deviant behaviors inasmuch as the initiation of risk behaviors during early adolescence is often a precursor for more serious delinquent behavior during late adolescence and adulthood (Gottfredson, 2001; Jessor, 1998; Loeber & Stouthamer-Loeber, 1987). As indicated previously, the present investigation attempts to address these issues by assessing the extent to which parental attachment, family socioeconomic status, and deviant peer relationships predict youth involvement in risk behaviors and delinquency among urban African American middle school students.

Theoretical Explanations of Youth Deviance

Over the years, eight theoretical perspectives have come to dominate the social science literature regarding youth deviance. The main tenets of each of these theories are briefly summarized as follows: 1) social learning – whereby deviance occurs as a result of intellectual and social skills deficits within the individual and such behavior is learned through associations with other individuals who themselves are deviant; 2) rational choice – whereby individuals perform rational calculations of risk versus reward and engage in deviant behaviors if rewards are considered to be high and risks are low; 3) structural functionalism – whereby deviant behavior exists within society as a result of social inequities and may serve the purpose of challenging the status quo while also maintaining and reinforcing social norms by rewarding conformists and punishing deviants; 4) conflict – whereby deviant behavior occurs as a result of opposing groups competing for scarce resources; 5) labeling – whereby youth who commit deviant acts are identified or labeled by members of society as being deviant, they then internalize this belief, as adolescence is a time when self-identifies are formed, thus increasing the likelihood that they will continue to engage in such behaviors in the future; 6) social control – whereby youth who are weakly attached to society are more likely to participate in deviant behaviors; 7) strain – whereby individuals in society share similar values and beliefs and strive for success through socially acceptable means to obtain desired resources, however, when individuals are blocked or restricted from obtaining such resources legitimately, internal conflicts may occur and participation in illegitimate or deviant acts may be viewed as a means to obtain such resources; and 8) cultural deviance – whereby the social and environmental conditions to which an individual is exposed determines their behavioral patterns and whether they will participate in deviant acts (Hoffmann, 2003; Leighninger, 1996; Rankin & Wells, 1990; Sullivan & Wilson, 1995).

Conceptual Framework

Hirschi's social control theory (1969) was chosen as the conceptual framework for the present study because of its emphasis on the role of early childhood socialization in connecting youth to society, the importance that it places on parental attachments in deterring youth involvement in risk behaviors and delinquency, and its widespread support and acceptance in delinquency research and theory (Hirschi, 1969; LaGrange & White, 1985; Marcos & Bahr, 1988; Pabon, 1998; Schaefer & Lamm, 1998; Tolan et al., 1986). The following sections discuss the role of early childhood socialization in connecting youth to society and the four elements of the social bond, as posited by Hirschi (1969), that deter youth involvement in deviant activities.

Early Childhood Socialization

According to Hirschi (1969), humans become social beings through the process of socialization, whereby previously established social standards of behavior are passed to successive generations by parents and other members of society. In its essence, socialization is the process by which individuals acquire an awareness of social stimuli and learn the proper way to behave and respond to social norms and influences in similar ways as others in their group or culture (McNeil, 1969). Thus, if individuals are appropriately socialized, they generally share the same norms and values as other members of society and frown upon individuals who deviate from accepted standards of behavior (Hirschi, 1969; Schaefer & Lamm, 1998). However, if individuals are inappropriately socialized, they may become weakly attached to society and thus may be less concerned about the opinions and expectations of others (Hirschi, 1969). Hence, they may become independent of social restrictions and be less inclined to follow social norms *freeing* themselves for participation in deviant behaviors (Hanlon, Bateman, Simon, O'Grady, & Carswell, 2002; Hirschi, 1969).

The Elements of the Social Bond

In his conceptualization of social control theory, Hirschi (1969) suggests that the social bond or the *glue* that maintains individual adherence to normative societal behavior is comprised of four elements: 1) attachment; 2) commitment; 3) involvement; and 4) beliefs. As most research utilizing Hirschi's social control theory (1969) has focused on the element of attachment and its relationship to youth delinquency (Haynie, 2001; Kempf, 1993; LeBlanc, 1992; Vold, Bernard, & Snipes, 1998) and because parental attachment in particular has been found to predict youth delinquency more consistently than other factors (Rosenbaum, 1989), the present study focused exclusively on the effect of this element on youth behavior. However, descriptions of each of the four elements that comprise the social bond and social control theory, itself, are briefly presented below. Central to Hirschi's conceptualization of the element of *attachment* is the critical role that the family plays in the establishment of pro-social bonds between child and society. According to Hirschi (1969), emotional and psychological bonds between parent and child are established during infancy as children rely on their parents for their care. It is during this period that parental values, beliefs, and expectations are passed to the child through the human socialization process (Hirschi, 1969; Rheingold, 1969). As children grow, parents maintain direct and indirect control over youth compliance to social norms through behavioral modification controls. Direct controls are maintained through a system of rewards and punishments with appropriate behavior being positively reinforced while inappropriate behavior is disapproved. On the other hand, indirect controls are maintained through previously established *affiliative* bonds between parent and child whereby the child values the parental relationship and shies away from acts that might lead to parental disapproval (Rankin & Wells, 1990; Smith & Stern, 1997). Moreover, according to Hirschi (1969), strong bonds between parent and child are established through good communication, parental supervision and discipline, and the child's ability to identify with their parents and through a desire to be like their parents (Akers, 1997; Hirschi, 1969; LeBlanc, 1992). However, according to Hirschi (1969), if the bond between parent and child is weak or broken, direct and indirect controls will lose their effectiveness, increasing the likelihood that youth will participate in deviant activities.

According to Hirschi (1969), the concept of parental attachment consists of three interrelated components: virtual supervision, intimacy of communication, and affectional identification. Virtual supervision pertains to the extent to which the parent is psychologically rather than physically present in the child's mind when they are tempted to participate in delinquent acts and whether these thoughts restrict their involvement in such activities. Intimacy of communication is the degree to which the child is comfortable sharing their thoughts and feelings with their parents, the amount of positive communication shared between them, and the child's comfortableness in being able to solicit advice and guidance from their parents. Affectional identification is the degree of closeness and connectedness that youth feel toward their parents and the extent to which the child desires to be like his or her parent when they become an adult. In addition, throughout the years, researchers have also used the following additional variables to measure the concept of parental attachment: 1) joint/leisure interpersonal involvement – the amount of time that youth spend with their parents in joint and/or leisure time activities; and 2) the child's acceptance of parental roles – the amount of respect youth have for their parents and the degree of acceptance they have for their parents' values and overall parenting styles (Akers, 1997; Pabon, 1998).

Operationally, virtual supervision has been measured through the summation of scores on the following types of questions: 1) Does your mother (father) know where you are when you are away from home; and 2) Does your mother (father) know whom you are with when you are away from home (Hirschi, 1969; Kempf, 1993). Intimacy of communication is measured through summed scores to the following types of questions: 1) Do you share your thoughts and feelings with your mother (father); and 2) How often have you talked over your future plans with your mother (father) (Hirschi, 1969; Kempf, 1993). Affectional identification has been measured by the response to the following type of question: 1) Would you like to be the kind of person your mother (father) is (Hirschi, 1969; Kempf, 1993). Joint/leisure time interpersonal involvement has been measured by responses to the following types of questions: 1) How often do you go to sports events with your parents; and 2) How often do you watch television with your parents (Hirschi, 1969). A child's acceptance of parental rules has been measured by responses to the following types of questions: 1) When you don't know why your mother (father) makes a rule, will she explain the reason; 2) When you come across things you don't understand, does your mother (father) help you with them; and 3) Does your mother (father) ever explain why she feels the way she does (Hirschi, 1969; Kempf, 1993). Across all dimensions, the weight attributed to the child's responses to these types of questions is of equal importance for both mother and father (Hirschi, 1969; Kempf, 1993).

Commitment refers to the degree to which an individual is integrated into the social activities and institutional arrangements of society (Hirschi, 1969). Intrinsic within Hirschi's conceptualization of commitment is the belief that delinquency is a function of the extent to which youth have personally invested their time in adhering to socially accepted practices and methods of procuring desired goods and services. As such, the more individuals invest their time, energy, and personal resources into the maintenance of socially acceptable behaviors and in attaining desired goods and services, the less likely they are to engage in deviant behaviors because the investment of one's personal time and the resulting resources accumulated would be too great a loss to risk engaging in deviant acts. However, those individuals who have invested less and who are less integrated into society are more likely to participate in such activities as they may feel they have more to gain and less to lose (Hirschi, 1969).

The third element of social bonding pertains to *involvement*, which refers to the belief that as a person commits more of himself or herself to the goal of obtaining socially desired goods and resources the more of their time they spend in such pursuits at the exclusion of those that are less desirable. In effect, investment of one's time, energy, and personal resources into those activities that are deemed socially acceptable and socially rewarding limit the amount of time available to participate in deviant behaviors (Hirschi, 1969). For example, individuals who are employed full-time are less likely to have sufficient spare time during the work day to engage in deviant acts because of the necessity to conform to a schedule in which their daily lives are structured around employment activities (Wilson, 1996).

Finally, the last element of Hirschi's social control theory (1969) relates to the extent to which an individual accepts the *belief* that society's norms and value systems are morally valid and personally meaningful. Consequently, those individuals who believe in society's moral and behavioral doctrines and standards are more likely to uphold them and far less likely to commit deviant acts than are those individuals who have weakly accepted these beliefs (Hirschi, 1969; Siegel & Senna, 1991).

Theoretical Critiques of Hirschi's Social Control Theory

Although Hirschi's social control theory (1969) has garnered significant empirical support throughout the years (Jensen & Rojek, 1992; Kempf, 1993; Lanier & Henry, 1998), advocates of alternate theoretical perspectives, which attempt to explain adolescent deviant behavior, do not necessarily agree with some of its underlying assumptions. For example, advocates of labeling theory argue that Hirschi's social control theory places too much emphasis on the various types of institutional social control and the ways in which such institutional controls link youth to conventional society through the socialization process, which in turn reduces youth participation in deviant activities (Lanier & Henry, 1998). Instead, proponents of this perspective argue that the institutional social controls themselves, specifically with respect to individuals in powerful positions, engender deviance through negative socialization (Lanier & Henry, 1998; Lilly, Cullen, & Ball, 1989). From this perspective, deviance occurs as a result of these powerful people overreacting to minor rule breaking by youth and their subsequent labeling of these youth as deviants. Such labeling not only undermines their feelings of self-worth but also results in the internalization of the belief that they are, in fact, deviants, thus, increasing the likelihood that they will engage or continue to engage in deviant acts (Lanier, 2003; Lilly, Cullen, & Ball, 1989). Thus, from the perspective of labeling theory, it is not the lack of bonding to conventional others resulting from inadequate socialization that leads youth to commit deviant acts. Rather, it is the labeling of mischievous youth as deviants, by the agents of societal institutions, which increases the likelihood that they will internalize such beliefs and continue to participate in deviant activities into the future (Lanier, 2003; Lilly, Cullen, & Ball, 1989).

Representing another viewpoint, advocates of general strain theory posit that Hirschi's social control theory (1969), has limited explanatory power with respect to youth delinquency (Agnew, 1985; Greenberg, 1999). Specifically, advocates of this theoretical perspective argue that the predictive value of social control theory is not as strong as initially implied in Hirschi's seminal work, *Causes of Delinquency*, and that additional factors, other than those outlined by social control theory but predicted by strain theory, provide a supplemental account for variations in youth involvement in delinquency (Agnew, 1985; Greenberg, 1999). For example, although Hirschi's social control theory (1969) can account for low social control related to youth involvement in negative or detached relationships and the subsequent delinquency that may be related to such events, strain theory supplements such accounts by positing that the underlying factor or related effect regarding youth involvement in such relationships is the experience of frustration and this frustration may lead to anger-based delinquency (Agnew, 1985). The proponents of general strain theory argue that, as such, Hirschi's social control theory has limited explanatory power in explaining youth delinquency and should be supplemented by strain theory to account for underlying strain factors, such as an experience of frustration, which may lead youth to participate in such activities (Agnew, 1985; Greenberg, 1999).

Study Rationale

Although an extensive amount of previous research has investigated relationships between parental attachment, deviant peer relationships, and youth involvement in deviant behaviors (Jensen & Rojek, 1992; Kempf, 1993; Lanier & Henry, 1998; Giordano & Cernkovich, 1993; Dishion, 1990; Dishion et al., 1995a, 1995b; Rankin & Quane, 2002), little empirical research has focused on the relationships between socioeconomic status, parental attachment, deviant peer relationships, and youth involvement in risk behaviors and delinquency (Bellair & Roscigno, 2000; Capaldi & Patterson, 1994; Fergusson, Swain-Campbell, & Horwood, 2004; LeBlanc, 1992; Wadsworth, 2000). As discussed earlier, youth participation in risk behaviors and delinquency are both serious problems in the United States (Farrington et al., 2002; Miller et al., 1998; Smith & Stern, 1997; Thornton et al., 2000), as empirical research has consistently demonstrated that if such behavior is left unchecked, its continuation may have life-long detrimental consequences for an individual's health and well-being, as these youth are likely to continue to participate in such activities into adulthood (Barnes & Welte, 1986; Grunbaum et al., 2002; Ingoldsby & Shaw, 2002; Jessor & Jessor, 1977; Newcomb, Maddahian, & Bentler, 1986). In particular, African American youth from disadvantaged urban communities, who are disproportionately exposed to serious social and environmental risk factors, initiation and continuation of such problematic behaviors may lead to early school failure, illicit drug use, violent behavior, and the occurrence of premature death (Duncan & Yeung, 1995; Grant et al., 2000; Huston, McLoyd, & Coll, 1994; Jessor, 1993; McLeod & Shanahan, 1993). Thus, considering the dangers and negative influences characterizing high-risk socially and economically disadvantaged urban neighborhoods, and the problems faced by adolescents living in such environments, research that investigates those factors that are strongly associated with youth involvement in risk behaviors and delinquency is sorely needed. The sections that follow immediately below further elaborate on the rationale for further investigation of specific aspects of this study.

Strength of Parental Attachment

Hirschi's social control theory (1969) has garnered substantial empirical support throughout the years and as such has become one of the predominant theories within delinquency research (Jensen & Rojek, 1992; Kempf, 1993; Lanier & Henry, 1998). However, some researchers contend that certain elements of the theory may not be as strong as Hirschi (1969) originally posited or that have been subsequently indicated by other researchers with respect to its predictive value concerning delinquency (Vold, Bernard, & Snipes, 2001; Greenberg, 1999). For example, Agnew (1991) contends that the element of attachment is only minimally associated with delinquency and that such associations are indirect. The research of Krohn and Massey (1980), also found that the element of attachment was the weakest predictor of delinquency within social control theory but that among the attachment foci, parental attachment was the most important factor in predicting delinquency (Krohn & Massey, 1980). Moreover, the reanalysis of selected tables within social control theory by Greenberg (1999) also questions the strength of parental attachment in explaining delinquency as findings from this work indicate, at best, small to moderate relationships. The preceding examples seemingly contradict previous work, which indicates that the element of attachment and more specifically parental attachment is an important deterrent to delinquency (Cernkovich & Giordano, 1987; Jensen & Rojek, 1992; Stern & Smith, 1995; Nye, 1958). Hence, because questions remain regarding the predictive value of parental attachment in explaining delinquency, additional work is needed to further clarify these relationships (Agnew, 1991).

Deviant Peer Relationships

Although an impressive body of research offers support for the view that strong parental attachments deter delinquency (Jensen & Rojek, 1992) and youth involvement in deviant peer relationships (Kandel & Andrews, 1987; Vitaro, Brendgen, & Tremblay, 2000; Warr 2005), other studies' findings suggest that deviant peer relationships are a stronger predictor of youth delinquency than the strength of parental attachments (Agnew, 1991; Elliott et al., 1985; Haynie, 2001; Warr & Stafford, 1991). For example, Warr (1993b) found that regardless of the strength of the relationship between parent and child, parental attachment did not reduce the positive association between deviant peer relationships and youth delinquency. Moreover, both Agnew's (1991) and Greenberg's (1999) research work concurs with these findings, suggesting that the influence of strong parental attachments in deterring youth involvement in risk behaviors and delinquency is significantly reduced as youth move into their teen years and peer influences become more important. Indeed, Hirschi (1969) noted that one of the limitations of social control theory was its underestimation of the importance of peer influences as he himself found that delinquency was most strongly associated with youth involvement in deviant peer relationships (Akers, 1997; Kempf, 1993). As such, additional research is warranted to investigate not only the possible association between deviant peer relationships and youth involvement in risk behaviors and delinquency but also to assess whether such relationships are a much stronger predictor of youth involvement in risk behaviors and delinquency than parental attachment.

Family Socioeconomic Status

In view of the discrepant findings regarding the extent to which family socioeconomic status differentially relates to youth delinquency at the individual and aggregate level, and because many prominent theories of crime and delinquency are based on the existence of a relationship between socioeconomic status and delinquency at the individual level, more definitive work is needed to determine the relationship between family socioeconomic status, parental attachment, and youth involvement in risk behaviors and delinquency. As previously indicated, recent empirical work has focused on delineating those specific circumstances in which the three are strongly correlated. One specific scientific inquiry (Bellair & Roscigno, 2000), employing stratification research, focused on the indirect links between socioeconomic status and delinquency through parental attachment. Although there is emerging empirical support for linkages among family socioeconomic status, parental attachment, and youth delinquency, conclusions must be tempered because evidence is still relatively sparse. However, the limited research that has been conducted in this area appears to indicate that investigations of such linkages would be both fruitful and meaningful in view of findings suggesting that lower socioeconomic status is related to weak parental attachment and indirectly associated with youth involvement in deviant behaviors (Bellair & Roscigno, 2000; LeBlanc, 1992).

Gender Considerations

Research suggests that consideration of gender differences is fundamental to an understanding of youth deviance (Chesney-Lind, 1986, 1997; Daly, 1994; Nichols, Graber, Brooks-Gunn, & Botvin, 2006; Piquero, Gover, MacDonald, & Piquero, 2005; Rhodes & Fischer; 1993; Sarigiani et al., 1999). Inasmuch as potential gender differences among African American males and females have not been clearly delineated with respect to their participation in deviant activities (Juon, Doherty, & Ensminger, 2006), further investigations of the plausible differential factors associated with their participation in such activities are warranted.

Summary

The present study attempts to further clarify the relationships among parental attachment, family socioeconomic status, deviant peer relationships, and youth involvement in risk behaviors and delinquency and to assess the type and extent of youth participation in such activities. In addition, this study will attempt to clarify the predictive value of parental attachment with respect to youth involvement in risk behaviors and delinquency. Moreover, this investigation will assess potential gender differences with respect to youth participation in such activities. Finally, this investigation will endeavor to expand upon previous work in delinquency research through its examination of African American family relations with respect to family attachment and how such attachments impact on youth involvement in risk behaviors and delinquency, as these are particularly understudied areas of scientific inquiry (Bell-Scott, 1990; Borduin et al., 2001; Giordano & Cernkovich, 1993; Kenny, Gallagher, Alvarez-Salvat, & Silsby, 2002; Rodney, Tachia & Rodney, 1999; McKenry et al., 1989; Smetana, Crean, & Daddis, 2002; Weber et al., 1995). Previous research regarding African American families has primarily focused its attention on aspects of family structure (Dickerson, 1995; Billingsley; 1992; Herskovits, 1941; Hill, 1997; Moynihan, 1965); neighborhood effects (Anderson, 1991; Crane, 1991; Duncan & Hoffman, 1991; Skogan, 1990); racism (Feagin & Vera, 1995; Shapiro, 2004; Wilson, 1980); social inequities and inequality (Jargowsky; 1997; Shapiro, 2004; Wilson, 1987, 1995); and social relations, resiliency, and coping strategies (Stack, 1974; Peters, 1997; Thornton & Coudert, 1995).

CHAPTER 3

Research Design and Analytic Framework

Study Design

A single-sample cross-sectional study design is being utilized for purposes of this investigation.

Sample Characteristics

Archival data were obtained on 536 urban African American students 12 – 14 years of age in 1998. The student sample consisted of 260 males (48.5%) and 276 females (51.5%), all of whom were enrolled in the sixth grade at one of two Baltimore City middle schools and who participated in an after-school program evaluation conducted by researchers at the Friends' Social Research Center (FSRC). Determined on a chance basis, one of the schools involved in the study served as the experimental and the other as the comparison site. In terms of the characteristics of the geographic areas and general populations served, the two sites were equally representative of higher risk urban settings.

Inclusion/Exclusion Criteria

Given the school districts of the two Baltimore City middle schools in which participant data were collected, it was anticipated that only a few non-African American students would likely be included in the data sample. Because one of this study's goals was to investigate African American family

49

dynamics in general and adolescent's relationships with parents, specifically, eight non-African American students, as self-defined by participant responses to questions regarding race/ethnicity, were dropped from the sample, resulting in a final sample of 536 students.

Measurement Instruments Administered to the Sample

Once enrolled in the after-school program, all participants were administered a set of baseline and follow-up assessment measures designed to assess parental attachment, family socioeconomic status, deviant peer relationships, and youth involvement in risk behaviors and delinquency. In the present investigation only data obtained from measures administered at baseline to students, parent (caregiver), and teachers were examined. A brief description of each of these measures is presented below.

Interview Questionnaires

Self-report information regarding youth was obtained by means of a structured interview schedule, the *Youth Self-Report Questionnaire* (YSRQ), which was developed and utilized in previous FSRC research with African American youth. This measure included questions about self-reported characteristics, circumstances, and experiences during adolescence. In addition to demographic information, the principal areas covered were parent and child relationships, school conduct and performance, the deviance of peer associates, and the extent of youth involvement in risk behaviors and delinquency. A parent (caregiver) was also administered a structured interview schedule, the *Parent*

(Caregiver) Self-Report Questionnaire (PSRQ), also utilized in previous FSRC research with the families of African American youth. This measure included questions about parent and child relationships, parental education, work experiences, and family income.

The Child Behavior Checklist (CBCL)

Completed by a caregiver, the CBCL (Achenbach & Edelbrock, 1987) is designed to assess in a standardized format the competencies and behavior/emotional problems of youth as reported by a parent (caregiver). The CBCL, which obtains both internalizing (psychological problems) and externalizing (conduct problems) standardized scores, has been widely used as a research instrument to assess children, and there is considerable published data regarding its reliability and validity (Bérubé & Achenbach, 2001).

Conners' Rating Scales-Revised (CRS-R)

The short version of this standardized instrument (Conners, 1997) was used to assess the conduct and emotional problems of the children from the separate viewpoints of their parent (caregiver) and teachers. The scales, which measure oppositional and cognitive problems as well as hyperactivity manifestations over the past month, provide pertinent behavioral information.

Teachers Report Form (TRF)

Completed by teachers, the TRF is designed to provide teachers' reports of their pupils adaptive functioning and problems in a standardized format (Achenbach, 1991).

Modeled on the CBCL, it provides an efficient and economical means of comparing a particular child's school functioning with the functioning of a normative sample of same-aged youth. As with the CBCL, it is possible to obtain internalizing and externalizing standardized scores.

Measures

The endogenous, exogenous, and control variables that were examined in this investigation, along with the variable scoring scheme, are described below and presented in table form (see **Tables 2**, **3**, and **4**, below). In structural equation modeling, an endogenous or dependent variable is a variable that changes as a result of the effect of one or more exogenous or other endogenous variables. An exogenous variable is a variable that brings about a change in one or more endogenous variables but is itself not caused by any other measured variables (Asher, 1983; Retherford & Choe, 1993).

Strictly Endogenous Variables

The two variables that served only as endogenous variables in this investigation were risk behaviors and delinquency.

Risk Behaviors

For purposes of this investigation, risk behaviors were defined as those acts that have been found to increase the likelihood of youth participation in deviant behaviors that may have both negative personal and social consequences (Hawkins et al., 1992, 1999; Kandel et al., 1986; Kirby & Fraser, 1997). The risk behavior score was a composite of four items which pertained to the involvement of youth in school performance problems (low attendance, low grades, grade repeat); school conduct problems (suspensions, expulsions); use of alcohol, tobacco and other drugs (ATODs); and early involvement in risky sexual activities (nature and extent of activity). When these individual scores were aggregated, a higher *total score* for risk behaviors was indicative of *higher* youth participation in risk behaviors.

To assess the extent to which youth have participated in risk behaviors, information obtained from youth, parent (caregiver), and teachers at baseline was used to define this variable (see **Measures**, above). (For a complete listing of the questions used with respect to risk behaviors, please see **Appendix B**.)

Delinquency

For purposes of this investigation, delinquency was operationally defined as those acts that are committed by individuals under the age of eighteen that violate the law or the norms of a society (Siegel & Senna, 1991). The delinquency score was a composite of four items pertaining to youth involvement in crimes of violence (e.g., shot at anyone, mugging, robbery); crimes against property or person (e.g., arson, vandalism, stealing, shoplifting, sexual assault); status offenses (e.g., running away from home, truancy from school, incorrigibility); and illicit drug possession and distribution. When these individual scores were aggregated, a higher *total score* for delinquency was indicative of *higher* youth participation in delinquency.

To assess the extent to which youth have participated in delinquency, information obtained from youth and their parent (caregiver) at baseline was used to define this variable (see **Measures**, above). (For a complete listing of the questions used with respect to delinquency, please see **Appendix B**.)

Exogenous and Endogenous Variables

The exogenous and endogenous variables in this research are parental attachment, family socioeconomic status, and deviant peer relationships.

Parental Attachment

The parental attachment score was a composite of five items and pertains to the extent to which youth and their parents are bonded to one another through the measurement of the following interrelated components virtual supervision; intimacy of communication; affectional identification; and joint/leisure interpersonal involvement.

For purposes of this investigation, parental attachment was defined as the extent to which youth and their parents are bonded (Hirschi, 1969) to one another and was assessed through the measurement of the following interrelated components: virtual supervision, intimacy of communication, affectional identification, and joint/leisure interpersonal involvement. As distinguished by Hirschi (1969), virtual supervision, intimacy of communication, and affectional identification were defined as follows: Virtual supervision pertains to the extent to which a parent was psychologically rather than physically present in the child's mind when they are tempted to participate in delinquent acts and whether such thoughts restrict their involvement in such activities. Intimacy of communication was the degree to which the child is comfortable sharing their thoughts and feelings with their parents, the amount of positive communication shared between them, and the child's comfortableness in being able to solicit advice and guidance from their parents. Affectional identification was the degree of closeness and connectedness that youth feel toward their parents and the extent to which the child desires to be like his or her parent when they become an adult. The final interrelated component, joint and leisure interpersonal involvement, was operationally defined, as it has been previously in the literature, as the amount of time that youth spend with their parents in joint and/or leisure time activities (Akers, 1997; Pabon, 1998).

As stated above, the parental attachment score was a composite of five items and pertains to the extent to which youth and their parents are bonded to one another through the measurement of the following interrelated components virtual supervision; intimacy of communication; affectional identification; and joint/leisure interpersonal involvement. When these individual scores were aggregated, a higher *total score* for parental attachment was indicative of *lower* parental attachment.

To assess the degree of parental attachment between youth and their parents, information obtained from youth at baseline was used to define this variable (see **Measures**, above). (For a complete listing of the questions used with respect to parental attachment, please see **Appendix B**.)

Family socioeconomic status

This concept is comprised of two important aspects, one concerned with resources, such as education, income, and wealth, and the other with social status or rank, such as one's social class (Bradley, 2002; McCarthy et al., 2000). The family socioeconomic score was a composite of parental education, parental occupation, and family income. When these individual scores were aggregated, a higher *total score* for family socioeconomic status was indicative of *lower* family socioeconomic status.

For purposes of this investigation, family socioeconomic status was operationally defined as a combination of parental education, occupation, and family income (Bradley, 2002; McCarthy et al., 2000). To assess family socioeconomic status, information obtained from a parent (caregiver) at baseline was used to define this variable (see **Measures**, above). (For a complete listing of the questions used with respect to family socioeconomic status, please see **Appendix B**.) A modified version of the Hollingshead Index of Social Position scale (Hollingshead, 1975) was used to measure family socioeconomic status (see **Table 4**, below).

Deviant peer relationships

A deviant peer relationship score indicates the involvement of youth, as self-defined, in relationships with peers who have participated in risk behaviors and/or delinquency. When these individual scores were aggregated, a higher *total score* for associations with deviant peers was indicative of *higher* youth involvement in deviant peer relationships. For purposes of this investigation, deviant peer relationships are operationally defined as the extent to which youth associate with peers who themselves have participated in risk behaviors and/or delinquent activities. To assess the extent to which youth have associated with peers who are deviant, information obtained from youth, a parent (caregiver), and teachers at baseline was used to define this variable (see

Measures, above). (For a complete listing of the questions used with respect to deviant peer relationships, please see **Appendix B**.)

Issues Regarding the Use of Existing Data

The present investigation utilizes existing data to assess the degree to which parental attachment, family socioeconomic status, and deviant peer relationships are related to the involvement of youth in risk behaviors and delinquency. The advantages of using existing data are numerous, including being more efficient and economical than collecting original survey information, providing the ability to analyze results obtained from large surveys without the expenditures of time that such undertakings would ordinarily require, and increasing the generalizability of research findings (Babbie, 1995, 2004; Sullivan, 1992). The main disadvantage of using existing data revolves around the question of validity. Besides the fact that such data are being analyzed for a different purpose than originally intended, the researcher must assess whether the questions being utilized appropriately measure the variables under examination (Babbie, 1995, 2004; Sampson & Laub, 1995; Sullivan, 1992). In the present investigation, such considerations were addressed in a twofold manner: the constructs, operational definitions, survey questions, and composite measures utilized were representative of those previously used in similar research (Chesney-Lind, 1997; Hawkins et al., 1992, 1999; Hirschi, 1969; Hollingshead, 1975; Kandel, et al., 1986; Kempf, 1993; Kirby & Fraser, 1997; Matherne & Thomas, 2001; Siegel & Senna, 1991; Smith & Stern, 1997); and a large number of representative questions were used to construct each measure (Robbers, 1999).

In order to assess the reliabilities of the composite indices used in the present study to measure the constructs under examination, Cronbach's internal consistency α was calculated and is presented along with a description of the items involved (see **Table 4**, below). The α levels ranged from .54 to .86, with scores near the higher range (e.g., above .70) suggesting adequate internal consistency of the index (Vogt, 1999). [The alpha level for family socioeconomic status is not presented in the table because the composite index used to measure this construct is based on a modified version of the Hollingshead Index of Social Position scale (Hollingshead, 1975) and as such α could not be calculated.]

Table 1.	
Endogenous and Exogenous Variable Operational Definitions	
Variables	**Operational Definitions**
1- Risk Behaviors	Those acts that have been found to increase the likelihood of youth participation in deviant behaviors that may have both negative personal and social consequences.
2- Delinquency	Those acts that are committed by individuals under the age of eighteen that violate the law or the norms of a society. These acts would include crimes of violence, crimes against property or person, status offenses, and illicit drug possession and/or distribution.
3- Parental Attachment	The extent to which youth and their parents are bonded to one another and comprised of four interrelated components.
a. Virtual supervision	The extent to which a parent is psychologically rather than physically present in the child's mind when they are tempted to participate in delinquent acts and whether such thoughts restrict their involvement in such activities.

Table 1. cont.	
Endogenous and Exogenous Variable Operational Definitions	
Variables	**Operational Definitions**
b. Intimacy of communication	The degree to which the child is comfortable sharing their thoughts and feelings with their parents, the amount of positive communication shared between them, and the child's comfortableness in being able to solicit advice and guidance from their parents.
c. Affectional identification	The degree of closeness and connectedness that youth feel toward their parents and the extent to which the child desires to be like his or her parent when they become an adult.
d. Joint/leisure involvement	The amount of time that youth spend with their parents in joint and/or leisure time activities.
4- Family Socioeconomic Status	A concept comprised of two important aspects, one concerned with resources, such as education, income, and wealth, and the other with social status or rank, such as one's social class. As such, it is defined as a combination of parental education, occupation, and family income.
5- Deviant Peer Relationships	The extent to which youth associate with peers whom themselves have participated in risk behaviors and/or delinquent activities.

Table 2.	
Endogenous and Exogenous Variables and Instruments	
Variables	**Instruments**
1) Risk Behaviors:	
a. School performance problems	YSRQ, CBCL, TRF
b. School conduct problems	YSRQ, CBCL, CRS-R, TRF
c. Use of ATODs	YSRQ, TRF
d. Early involvement in risky sex	YSRQ

Table 2. cont.	
Endogenous and Exogenous Variables and Instruments	
Variables	**Instruments**
2) Delinquency:	
a. Crimes of violence	YSRQ
b. Crimes against property/person	YSRQ, CBCL
c. Status offenses	YSRQ, CBCL
d. Illicit drug possession/distribution	YSRQ, TRF
3) Parental Attachment:	
a. Virtual supervision	YSRQ
b. Intimacy of communication	YSRQ
c. Affectional identification	YSRQ
d. Joint/leisure involvement	YSRQ
4) Family Socioeconomic Status:	
a. Parental education	PSRQ
b. Parental occupation	PSRQ
c. Family income	PSRQ
5) Deviant Peer Relationships:	
a. Associations with deviant peers	YSRQ, CBCL, TRF

Note: CBCL = Child Behavior Checklist; CRS-R = Conners' Rating Scales Revised; PSRQ = Parent Self-Report Questionnaire; TRF = Teacher's Report Form; and YSRQ = Youth Self-Report Questionnaire.

Table 3.	
Endogenous and Exogenous Variable Question Types	
Variables	**Types of Questions**
1) Risk Behaviors:	
a. School performance problems	1) Have you ever gotten into trouble because of attendance?
b. School conduct problems	2) Have you ever been suspended from school?
c. Use of ATODs	3) Have you ever had a drink of beer, wine, or liquor?
d. Early involvement in risky sex	4) Have you ever had sexual activity with someone

Table 3. cont.	
Endogenous and Exogenous Variable Question Types	
Variables	**Types of Questions**

2) Delinquency:
   a. Crimes of violence
   b. Crimes against property/person
   c. Status offenses
 	
   d. Illicit drug possession/ distribution
	1) Have you ever mugged anyone?
	2) Have you ever damaged or destroyed property that did not belong to you?
	3) Have you ever stayed out all night without permission?
	4) Have you ever sold drugs?

3) Parental Attachment:
   a. Virtual supervision
 	
   b. Intimacy of communication
   c. Affectional identification
 	
   d. Joint/leisure involvement
	1) When you leave the house during the day, do you have to tell anyone where you're going and when you'll be back?
	2) You enjoy talking things over with your mother/father?
	3) Would you like to be the kind of person your mother/father is when you're grown up?
	4) About how often does/do your parent(s) take you out just for fun or recreation?

4) Family Socioeconomic Status:
   a. Parental education
 	
   b. Parental occupation
 	
   c. Family income
	1) What was the last year of education that you completed?
	2) Over the past year, what have you done for a living?
	3) What would you estimate your annual household income to be?

5) Deviant Peer Relationships: a. Associations with deviant peers	1) Have any of your close friends ever been expelled from school?

Table 4.

Endogenous and Exogenous Variable Scoring Scheme

Variables	# of Items	Score (No/Yes)
1) Risk Behaviors (α = .77):		
a. School performance problems	11	(0-11)
b. School conduct problems	8	(0-08)
c. Use of ATODs	6	(0-06)
d. Early involvement in risky sex	1	(0-01)
Possible Total Scores		**(0-26)**
2) Delinquency (α = .67):		
a. Crimes of violence	3	(0-03)
b. Crimes against property/person	14	(0-14)
c. Status offenses	3	(0-03)
d. Illicit drug possession/distribution	5	(0-05)
Possible Total Scores		**(0-25)**
3) Parental Attachment (α = .54):		
a. Virtual supervision	5	(0-05)
b. Intimacy of communication	8	(0-08)
c. Affectional identification	8	(0-08)
d. Joint/leisure involvement	2	(0-02)
Possible Total Scores		**(0-23)**
4) Family Socioeconomic Status:		
a. Parental education		
Professional Degree = 1		
Four-year College Graduate = 2		
One to three years college and business school = 3		
High School Graduate/GED or less = 4		
Possible Total Scores	**(1-4)**	

Variables	# of Items	Score (No/Yes)
Table 4. cont.		
Endogenous and Exogenous Variable Scoring Scheme		

4) Family Socioeconomic Status: cont.

    b. Parental occupation

             Higher Execs and Major Professionals = 1
             Business Mgrs, Admin, and Lesser Pros = 2
             Small Bus Owners, Clerical, Techs, Sales = 3
             Skilled Manual Employees = 4
             Semi-Skilled = 5
             Unskilled employees = 6
             Homemaker = 7
             Student, disabled, no occupation = 8

Possible Total Scores   **(1-8)**

Index of Social Position Total Score =
(Education score X 4) + (Occupation score X 8)

    c. Family income

           Above $50,000 = 1
           Above $40,000 but below $50,000 = 2
           Above $30,000 but below $40,000 = 3
           Above $20,000 but below $30,000 = 4
           Above $10,000 but below $20,000 = 5
           Below $10,000 = 6

Possible Total Scores   **(1-6)**

Family Income Score = (Income score X 6)

Socioeconomic Status Index Score =
(Index of Social Position Total Score) + (Family Income Score

Possible Total Scores   **(3-116)**

Table 4. cont.		
Endogenous and Exogenous Variable Scoring Scheme		
Variables	**# of Items**	**Score (No/Yes)**
5) Deviant Peer Relationships (α = .86):		
a. Associations with deviant peers	20	(0-20)
Possible Total Scores		**(0-20)**

Note: Except for the Socioeconomic Status and Parental Attachment Index, a higher score on an index indicates a higher level of the underlying dimension involved. For the Socioeconomic and Parental Attachment Index, a higher score is indicative of lower Socioeconomic Status and lower Parental Attachment, respectively.

Hypotheses

In the present investigation, a structural equation modeling approach that specifies the relationships among parental attachment, family socioeconomic status, deviant peer relationships and risk behaviors and delinquency will be utilized. Using such an approach, hypotheses are not stated outside of the models, as the competing hypothesized structural equation models themselves are the hypotheses and such models are being evaluated to assess their ability to explain the observed data. Thus, in structural equation modeling, the model contains a series of hypotheses and competing hypothetical models are being tested that express the putative cause and effect relationships among a set of variables. These competing models are fit to the data and tested to determine which one best explains the observed data. As such, in this investigation, the hypotheses of interest are presented in Figure 1 below and the hypothesized relationships among the variables are stated within the model descriptions (see **Alternative Structural Equation Models**, below).

Statistical Method

Structural Equation Modeling (SEM)

Structural equation modeling (Asher, 1983; Jöreskog & Sörbom, 1984, 1996; Retherford & Choe, 1993) was used to test an observed variable model that explains the putative causal links between parental attachment, family socioeconomic status, deviant peer relationships, and youth involvement in risk behaviors and delinquency. SEM is a very general multivariate statistical technique that has been used for both developing and testing theories in the social and behavioral sciences (Anderson, 1987; Mulaik, 1987; StatSoft, 2004). SEM is considered a relatively "new" statistical method, as compared to regression and factor analysis, as this technique did not initially appear in research papers until the late 1960s (StatSoft, 2004). SEM is known by a variety of names in the literature, including covariance structure analysis, causal modeling, and path analysis, and, as it assumes that causal relationships exist between predictor and response variables, the relationships between such variables must be clearly defined (Babbie, 1995, 2004; Retherford & Choe, 1993). SEM is considered to be a more powerful, alternative statistical technique compared to factor analysis and time series analysis (Bentler & Chou, 1987; StatSoft, 2004) and it has a number of key advantages over more traditional statistical techniques such as ordinary least squares and multiple regression, including the following: 1) SEM requires the researcher to state as precisely as possible a hypothesized model or models that explain the relationships among all the variables under examination, 2) SEM allows for the simultaneous estimation of these relationships, by estimation methods such as maximum likelihood; and, 3) Given the possibility of a lack of fit of a hypothesized model or models, various methods exist to compare the fit of competing models, to diagnose the cause or causes of lack of fit, and to help determine plausible replacement or rival models that might better explain the observed data (StatSoft, 2004).

Within SEM, path diagrams are generally used to graphically depict the hypothesized causal relationships between variables, which are derived from theory and not from the observed data (Anderson, 1987; Retherford & Choe, 1993), with straight and/or dotted lines and arrows being used in these diagrams to indicate direct and alternative causal pathways and relationship patterns (see **Figure 1**, below). However, it is important to note that it is unlikely that any structural model will perfectly fit the data being analyzed, in view of the fact that a hypothesized model is only an approximation of social reality. As such, a model should be evaluated in terms of its ability to provide a close approximation of reality and its ability to offer plausible explanations of data trends and relationship patterns that are readily apparent during data analysis (StatSoft, 2004).

Estimation Method

Various methods of estimation of the parameters for the models depicted in Figure 1 have been proposed and discussed in the literature, including maximum likelihood (ML), generalized least squares (GLS), and various weighted least squares or asymptotic distribution free (WLS/ADF) methods (Muthén & Satorra, 1995; Olsson, Foss, Troye, & Howell, 2002). However, it is difficult to draw firm conclusions in regard to the ideal choice of methods of estimation, as considerable empirical research on this issue still needs to be conducted. However, ML estimates are consistent and efficient, and appear to be surprisingly insensitive to at least some forms of non-normality in the data, within a reasonable range of sample sizes, and thus ML estimation would seem to yield parameter estimates that are more accurate than other methods (Olsson et al., 2002). Therefore, ML estimation methods were utilized in the current study. The χ^2 tests of model fit and standard errors of the parameter estimates were based on robust methods. Muthén and Satorra (1995) have shown that the effects of both non-normality and non-independence of the observed data on such tests of significance and standard errors are negligible, even in the case of complex sampling designs.

Model Fit

Although the choice of which goodness-of-fit statistic to report in SEM analysis is somewhat arbitrary (Brough & Frame, 2004), based on recommendations in the literature (Bentler, 1990; Bollen, 1989; Brough & Frame, 2004; Donohew et al., 1999; Hu and Bentler, 1999; Iriondo, Albert, & Escudero, 2003; Marsh & Hocevar, 1985; Vogt, 1999; Wheaten, Muthen, Alwin, & Summers, 1977), six criteria were used to evaluate goodness-of-fit for each of the models under investigation: 1) chi-square test of significance of the hypothesized model; 2) chi-square/degrees of freedom; 3) normed fit index (*NFI*); 4) comparative fit index (*CFI*); 5) standardized root mean squared residual (*SRMR*); and 6) root mean square error of approximation (*RMSEA*). Previous research suggests that in most instances high χ^2 values for tests of model fit are indications of poor model fit (Brough & Frame, 2004). However, because large χ^2 values are in part reflective of the number of variables in the model, the complexity of the model, and the number of parameters estimated in the model, χ^2 can be divided by its degrees of freedom (*df*) to produce a relative chi-square statistic (Brough & Frame, 2004; Wheaten et al., 1977). The closer this statistic is to unity the better the fit, with results of up to five being an indication of reasonable fit, although a score of less than two is generally preferred (Brough & Frame, 2004; Marsh & Hocevar, 1985). Another method of assessing goodness-of-fit for SEM models is by evaluating the *NFI*, *CFI*, *SRMR*, and *RMSEA* values. These values depict how well a model fits a particular dataset (Vogt, 1999). If the *NFI* and *CFI* values are greater than .95 and the *SRMR* value is low (< .08) this typically reflects good model fit (Donohew et al., 1999; Hu and Bentler, 1999; Iriondo, Albert, & Escudero, 2003; Vogt, 1999). Finally, *RMSEA* (Browne & Cudeck, 1993; Donohew et al., 1999) is another method to evaluate goodness-of-fit for SEM models. Values equal to zero are generally accepted as being an indication of an exact model fit for the data (Donohew et al., 1999). For those *RMSEA* values higher than zero, Browne and Cudeck (1993) posited that values of .05 are indicative of close fit, .08 of marginal fit, and .10 of poor fit, taking into account degrees of freedom (Donohew et al., 1999).

Alternative Structural Equation Models

Alternative structural equation models may be used within

SEM to estimate and test the comparative fit of two or more competing structural models that are drawn from the literature (StatSoft, 2004). This is one of the major strengths of SEM, because the researcher is not simply limited to testing the adequacy of a single hypothetical model but instead has the ability to fit various models to the data, and compare the relative strengths of the various models to explain the observed data (Statsoft, 2004).

The principle that underlies specifying and testing competing models is that the researcher is strictly limiting his/her evaluation of hypothesized models to a restricted set of possible models that might have given rise to the data; therefore, the researcher can have substantial confidence in the results of his/her analyses, if one such model is supported. Although it is the typical belief that one of the hypothesized models will produce a reasonable fit to the data, model modification is often necessary, as many SEM researchers have noted that there are few instances in which a specified model is found to adequately fit the data (Statsoft, 2004). Therefore, it is often necessary to undertake data-driven revisions to one or more of the proposed models in order to find a conceptual model that more adequately explains observed data. However, as it is recognized that models resulting from such data-driven efforts have more tenuous support than do *a priori* specified models that are supported by statistical analysis, it is important to be mindful of these considerations when examining such *a posteriori* models.

Model Modification

The question of model modification following the rejection of the proposed models is an important issue to address. The proposed models introduced in this investigation as well as the various alternate models are somewhat complex and the empirical data in support of several paths in both hypothesized and alternate models is quite sparse or not compelling. Thus, it is quite likely that the hypothesized and proposed competing models will be rejected. As has been noted since the introduction of SEM (Jöreskog, 1971; Jöreskog & Sörbom, 1983), it is doubtful that *any* substantive SEM model that is proposed within the social and behavioral sciences can be so specified that it will not be rejected. Theories in the social and behavioral sciences are incomplete, and research to justify a given hypothesis is often not available or is contradictory.

The goal of model modification is to develop a substantive model that will help to explicate the phenomena under investigation. A substantive model is one that allows for the interpretation of the various paths in the model producing the best plausible explanation for observed data trends. However, in an effort to achieve this goal, one may modify the model by removing hypothesized causal paths that prove not to be significant and add paths that are significant, but in so doing, the resulting model may not be the model that gave rise to the sample data. Although there has been considerable attention paid to this issue in the SEM literature (e.g., Marcoulides, Drezner, & Schumacker, 1998), there is apparently no universal agreement regarding how one should proceed to modify a model in the face of its rejection.

The approach used in this investigation was similar to that described by Green and Babyak (1997), in that, model modification proceeded in two stages. In the first stage, paths were added to the model guided primarily by the theoretical consequences of a path and/or insights suggested by previous research. In addition, model modification involved the use of the Lagrange multiplier (LM) tests, if suggestions provided by such tests were sensible and produced a conceptually adequate model (Dunn, Everitt & Pickles, 1993). [The Lagrange multiplier (LM) test evaluates restrictions imposed on a model and provides suggestions with respect to freeing fixed parameters that could improve model fit. The LM tests also provide the change in the chi-square value that result from freeing each fixed parameter (Dunn, Everitt & Pickles, 1993).] In the second stage, any path was removed from the resulting modified model that was found to be non-significant when compared to $\alpha = .05$.

Proposed Models

In the present investigation, Model 4a (see **Figure 1**, below) is presented as the proposed model that is believed to offer the best fit for the data being examined in terms of its ability to provide plausible explanations of hypothesized variable relationships. For comparison purposes, alternative competing models depicted as Model 1, Model 1a, Model 2, Model 2a, Model 3, Model 3a, and Model 4 (see **Figure 1**, below) were evaluated. In Figure 1, the *double-headed* arrows in the diagram that point from one variable to another are expressions of unexamined correlations among the variables. Also, in Figure 1, the *single-headed* arrows that point from one variable to another are expressions of hypothesized direct causal relationships among the variables. In addition, an instance in which the effect of a variable is transmitted through an intervening variable indicates a hypothesized indirect causal relationship among the variables with the intervening variable being described as a mediating variable.

It is also being proposed that *within* Models 1, 2, 3, and 4 (see **Figure 1**, below) there may exist plausible alternative causal relationships among the variables. These relationships are depicted in Models 1a-4a (see **Figure 1**, below). As such, single-headed arrows with broken lines represent these proposed *within-model* possible alternative relationships. Summaries of the proposed direct, indirect, and within-model alternative hypothesized causal relationships among the variables, are described after the figure.

Figure 1. Predicted Path Models of Exogenous and Endogenous Variable Relationships

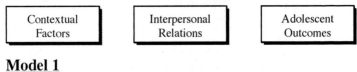

Model 1

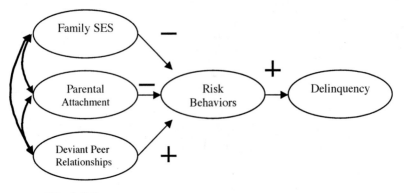

Model 1a

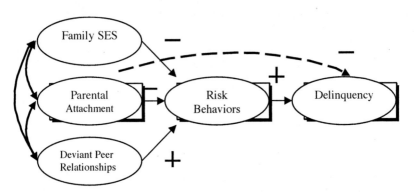

Contextual Factors	Interpersonal Relations	Adolescent Outcomes

Model 2

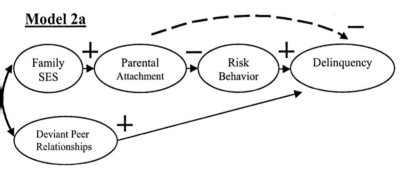

Model 2a

Contextual Factors	Interpersonal Relations	Adolescent Outcomes

Model 3

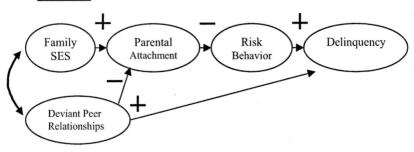

Model 3a

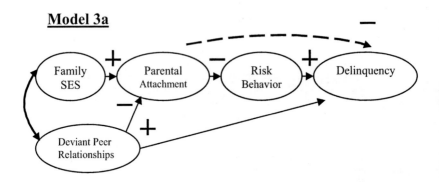

Model 4

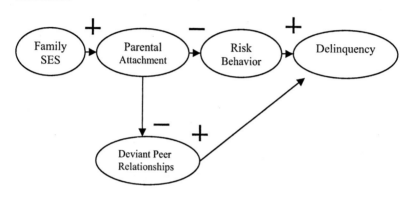

Model 4a

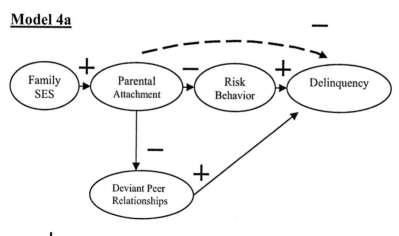

Note: ✚ = positive relationships while ▬ = negative relationships,
SES= socioeconomic status

Model 1 posits that family socioeconomic status, parental attachment, and deviant peer relationships are each directly related to risk behaviors. Although in structural terms, family socioeconomic status is directly related to risk behaviors, the relationship is an inverse one, that is, increasing family socioeconomic status implies a reduction in risk behaviors. Moreover, parental attachment is directly related to risk behaviors, although again, the relationship is an inverse one that is, increasing parental attachment is associated with a reduction in risk behaviors. Finally, deviant peer relationships are directly related to risk behaviors, in that, increasing deviant peer relationships is associated with an increasing in risk behaviors. In turn, risk behaviors are directly related to delinquency, such that, increasing risk behaviors is associated with an increasing in delinquency. Model 1 implies that family socioeconomic status, parental attachment, and deviant peer relationships are indirectly related to delinquency, through their respective relationship with risk behaviors, as the effect of these variables is transmitted through risk behaviors to delinquency. Thus, risk behaviors can be considered the single mediating variable in this model.

Model 1a, a variant of Model 1, posits an additional *alternative* hypothesized direct causal relationship between parental attachment and delinquency, such that parental attachment is directly related to delinquency, although the relationship is an inverse one, that is, increasing parental attachment implies a reduction in delinquency. The single-headed arrow with broken lines pointing from parental attachment to delinquency represents this proposed alternative hypothesized direct causal relationship.

Model 2 posits that family socioeconomic status is directly related to parental attachment, such that increasing family socioeconomic status implies increasing parental attachment. Family socioeconomic status is indirectly related to risk behaviors through its respective relationship with parental attachment, as the effect of this variable is transmitted through parental attachment to risk behaviors. In contrast, deviant peer relationships are directly related to risk behaviors, such that, increasing deviant peer relationships is associated with an increasing in risk behaviors. In turn, risk behaviors are directly related to delinquency, such that, increasing risk behaviors is associated with an increasing in delinquency. Thus, both parental attachment and risk behaviors can be considered mediating variables in this model. This model implies that family socioeconomic status is indirectly related to delinquency through its respective relationship with parental attachment and risk behaviors, as the effect of family socioeconomic status is transmitted through parental attachment to risk behaviors to delinquency. Deviant peer relationships are also indirectly related to delinquency through its direct relationship with risk behaviors, as the effect of this variable is transmitted through risk behaviors to delinquency. This model also posits that parental attachment is directly related to risk behaviors, although the relationship is an inverse one, such that increasing parental attachment is associated with a reduction in risk behaviors. In turn, risk behaviors are directly related to delinquency. Parental attachment is also indirectly related to delinquency through its respective relationship with risk behaviors, as the effect of this variable is transmitted through risk behaviors to delinquency. Thus, in contrast to Model 1, Model 2 posits an "indirect causal chain" from family socioeconomic status to parental attachment to risk behaviors and finally to delinquency.

Model 2a, a variant of Model 2 and similar to Model 1a, posits an additional *alternative* hypothesized direct causal relationship between parental attachment and delinquency, such that parental attachment is directly related to delinquency, although again this relationship is an inverse one, that is, increasing parental attachment is associated with a reduction in delinquency. The single-headed arrow with broken lines pointing from parental attachment to delinquency represents this proposed alternative hypothesized direct causal relationship.

Model 3 can be seen as a modification of Model 2 that posits an additional direct path from deviant peer relationships to parental attachment, although the relationship is an inverse one, such that increasing deviant peer relationships is associated with a reduction in parental attachment. All other variable relationships in Model 3 are similar to those previously described in Model 2.

Model 3a, a variant of Model 3 and similar to Model 2a, posits an additional *alternative* hypothesized direct causal relationship between parental attachment and delinquency, such that parental attachment is directly related to delinquency although the relationship is an inverse one, that is, increasing parental attachment is associated with a reduction in delinquency. The single-headed arrow with broken lines pointing from parental attachment to delinquency represents this proposed alternative hypothesized direct causal relationship.

Model 4 can be seen as a modification of Model 3, in which the path from deviant peer relationships to parental attachment is now reversed, with parental attachment posited as a cause of deviant peer relationships, rather than as a result of deviant peer relationships, as it is viewed in Model 3. As such, parental attachment is directly related to deviant peer relationships, although the relationship is an inverse one, that is, increasing parental attachment is associated with a reduction in deviant peer relationships. All other variable relationships in Model 4 are similar to those previously described in Model 3.

Model 4a, a variant of Model 4 and similar to Model 3a, posits an additional *alternative* hypothesized direct causal relationship between parental attachment and delinquency, such that parental attachment is directly related to delinquency although the relationship is an inverse one, that is, increasing parental attachment is associated with a reduction in delinquency. The single-headed arrow with broken lines pointing from parental attachment to delinquency represents this proposed alternative hypothesized direct causal relationship.

Model Implications

The descriptions of the hypothesized relationships in Models 1, 2, 3, and 4 (see **Figure 1**, above), reflect putative cause-and-effect relationships among the endogenous and exogenous variables as suggested by Hirschi's social control theory (1969) and previous research findings concerning the nature of such relationships (Bellair & Roscigno, 2000; Chaiken & Chaiken, 1990; Gottfredson, 1987; Greenberg, 1999; Kandel, 1986; Loeber & LeBlanc, 1990; Patterson et al., 2000). In addition, across all four models there exist invariant direct causal relationships (i.e., those variable relationships that are consistent across the models), which will impact on model analysis and interpretation. Across Models 1, 2, 3, and 4, parental attachment is directly although inversely related to risk behaviors. Parental attachment is also indirectly related to delinquency, as predicted by previous research findings (Bellair & Roscigno, 2000; Hirschi, 1969; LeBlanc, 1992; Stanton et al., 2002; Wadsworth, 2000). Moreover, deviant peer relationships are directly related to risk behaviors, such that increasing deviant peer relationships is associated with an increasing in risk behaviors (Beier et al., 2000; Keenan, Loeber, Zhang, Stouthamer-Loeber, & Van Kammen, 1995; Elliott et al., 1985, 1989; Matsueda & Anderson, 1998, Stanton, et al., 2002). Across Models 2, 3 and 4 there exists an invariant direct. causal relationship between family socioeconomic status and parental attachment with family socioeconomic status seen as a direct cause of parental attachment. Finally, across all four models, risk behaviors are directly related to delinquency, again, as suggested by previous research findings (Chaiken & Chaiken, 1990; Gottfredson, 1987; Loeber & LeBlanc, 1990; Vega et al., 1993).

Across all four models there also exist invariant indirect causal relationships. For example, across all four models family socioeconomic status, parental attachment, and deviant peer relationships are indirectly related to delinquency through their respective relationship with risk behaviors, as the effects of these variables are transmitted through risk behaviors to delinquency. Moreover, in Models 2, 3, and 4, family socioeconomic status is indirectly related to risk behaviors through its respective relationship with parental attachment, as the effect of this variable is transmitted through parental attachment to risk behaviors.

Across the four models, there also exist variant direct causal relationships (i.e., those variable relationships that are not consistent across the models), which will impact on model interpretation. For example, Model 1, in contrast to Models 2, 3, and 4, posits that family socioeconomic status is directly related to risk behaviors, although the relationship is an inverse one, such that increasing family socioeconomic status is associated with decreasing risk behaviors. In addition, Models 2, 3, and 4, in contrast to Model 1, posits that family socioeconomic status is directly related to parental attachment, such that increasing family socioeconomic status is directly related to increasing parental attachment. Moreover, Model 3, in contrast to Models 1, 2, and 4, posits a direct causal relationship between deviant peer relationships and parental attachment, although the relationship is an inverse one, such that increasing deviant peer relationships is associated with decreasing parental attachment. Finally, Model 4, in contrast to Models 1, 2, and 3, posits a direct causal relationship between parental attachment and deviant peer relationships, although the relationship is an inverse one, such that increasing parental attachment is associated with decreasing deviant peer relationships.

Across all four models there also exist variant indirect causal relationships. For example, Model 2, in contrast to Model 1, posits that family socioeconomic status is indirectly related to risk behaviors through its respective relationship with parental attachment, as the effect of this variable is transmitted through parental attachment to risk behaviors. In addition, Model 3, in contrast to Models 1, 2, and 4, posits that deviant peer relationships are indirectly related to parental attachment, as the effect of this variable is transmitted through parental attachment to risk behaviors. Finally, Model 4, in contrast to Models 1, 2, and 3, posits that parental attachment is indirectly related to risk behaviors through its respective relationship with deviant peer relationships, as the effect of this variable is transmitted through deviant peer relationships to risk behaviors.

CHAPTER 4

Summary of Findings

Descriptive Statistics

Table 5 provides the means, standard deviations, and Pearson product-moment correlations of the five variables specified in the structural models. The correlation coefficients used provides a measure of the degree to which two variables are related, ranging from -1 to $+1$ (Pallant, 2001; Vogt, 1999). A value of -1 is an indication of a perfect negative correlation such that if x is high then y is low, and vice versa. A value of $+1$ is an indication of a perfect positive correlation such that if x is high then y is high, and vice versa. A value of 0 is an indication that no relationship exists between the variables (Pallant, 2001; Vogt, 1999). In terms of assessing the strength of the relationship between variables, Cohen (1988) suggests the following scheme for the degree of relationship: $r = .10$ to $.29$ or $r = -.10$ to $-.29$ – small; $r = .30$ to $.49$ or $r = -.30$ to $-.49$ – medium; and $r = .50$ to 1 or $r = -.50$ to -1 – large.

The correlation coefficients are similar to previous findings in the literature regarding the variables examined (Agnew, 1991; Paschall, Ringwalt, & Flewelling, 2003; Rankin & Kern, 1994). With respect to the relationship between family socioeconomic status and youth participation in non-serious delinquency (e.g., drinking beer, smoking marijuana, truancy, etc.), Rankin and Kern (1994), using a racially and ethnically diverse sample of 1395 study participants that was 13% African-American, reported a positive relationship between the two ($r = .08$) such that lower socioeconomic status was related to higher youth involvement in non-serious delinquency. The present findings are similar to the previous findings in terms of the strength and direction of the relationship in that lower family socioeconomic status was related to higher youth participation in risk behaviors ($r = .14$).

With respect to the relationship between parental attachment and total delinquency, Rankin and Kern (1994) also reported a negative relationship between the two in regard to father ($r = -.32$) and mother attachment ($r = -.36$) such that higher parental attachment was related to lower youth participation in delinquent activities. This result is somewhat stronger than the correlation found in the present investigation in that lower parental attachment was only weakly related to higher youth participation in delinquent activities ($r = .16$). The present findings are not as strong as the correlations found in the previous findings in that lower parental attachment was only weakly related to higher youth participation in delinquent activities ($r = .16$).

With respect to the relationship between parental attachment and associations with deviant peers, Agnew (1991), using a racially and ethnically diverse sample of 1,725 study participants, reported a negative relationship between the two ($r = -.23$) such that higher parental attachment was related to lower associations with deviant peers. The present findings are similar to the previous findings in that lower parental attachment was related to higher associations with deviant peers ($r = .13$).

With respect to the relationship between associations with deviant peers and participation in delinquent activities, Paschall et al.'s (2003) research with 217 African American male adolescents in 1996 reported a positive relationship between the two ($r = .55$) such that higher associations with deviant peers was related to higher youth involvement in delinquent activities. The present findings are similar to the previous findings in terms of the strength and direction of the relationship in that higher association with deviant peers was related to higher participation in delinquent activities ($r =$ .41).

With respect to the relationship between non-serious delinquency and total delinquency, Rankin and Kern (1994), using a racially and ethnically diverse sample of 1395 study participants that was 13% African-American, reported a positive relationship between the two ($r = $ .84) in which higher non-serious delinquency was related to higher total delinquency. This result is similar to the correlation found in the present investigation in terms of the direction of the relationship in that higher youth participation in risk behaviors (indicative of non-serious deviant behavior) was related to higher youth participation in delinquency ($r = $.43).

African American Extended Family Networks

Extended family members often play an important role in African American families by providing support and assistance to parents in helping them raise positive-minded, healthy children (Billingsley, 1992; Collins, 1991; George & Dickerson, 1995; Hill, 1997). In some families, extended family members, particularly grandparents, may bear primary responsibility for rearing, caring, and protecting children when one or both birth parents are unavailable (Billingsley, 1992; Hill, 1997). Thus, one should be mindful of such considerations when investigating relationships between parental attachment and youth participation in risk behaviors and delinquency among African American youth.

With respect to the findings from this study, youth indicated that their birthmothers (82%) and birthfathers

(64%) were the individuals who had been acting as their mother and father for the longest time in their lives and who were primarily responsible for raising them. However, for some youth, extended family members also played prominent roles in their lives as grandmothers (11%), aunts (3%), and stepmothers (2%) had been acting as their mothers for the longest time in their lives. Moreover, for some youth, stepfathers (10%), grandfathers (5%), mother's boyfriends (5%), and uncles (4%) had been acting as their fathers for the longest time in their lives. Although these results indicate that for the majority of youth, birthmothers and birthfathers were the individuals who were primarily responsible for raising them, for some, extended family members played prominent roles in their lives as they had been acting as birthmother or birthfather when these individuals were not performing such duties.

Table 5. *Simple Correlations and Descriptive Statistics*

	SES	PA	AWDP	RB	DQ
SES					
PA	-.043	.054			
AWDP	.072	.129	.086		
RB	.143	.079	.331	.077	
DQ	.081	.157	.413	.427	.067
M	73.00	6.63	1.99	5.29	1.31
SD	20.34	2.82	2.97	3.83	1.57
Possible Range	3-116	0-23	0-20	0-32	0-25

Note: SES = Socioeconomic Status; PA = Parental Attachment; AWDP = Associations with Deviant Peers; RB = Risk Behaviors; and DQ = Delinquency. In addition, M = Mean; and SD = Standard Deviation.

Fit of the Models

Results of fitting the four proposed models and their alternatives can be found in **Table 6**, below. Based on the recommended criteria outlined above with respect to goodness-of-fit, all proposed models were rejected because their χ^2 values and relative chi-square statistics were both high, their Normed Fit Index (*NFI*) and Comparative Fit Index (*CFI*) values were always less than .95, and their Root Mean Square Error of Approximation (*RMSEA*) values were greater than .10. Although some model values met the Standardized Root Mean Squared Residual (*SRMR*) criterion (< .08) for good model fit, nevertheless, all models were rejected, because they failed to meet the remaining five of the six criteria set forth previously (see **Model Fit**, above) with respect to goodness-of-fit. Taken together, these statistics are indications of poor model fit.

Model Modification

Because none of the hypothesized models and their alternatives fit the observed data, it was necessary to engage in model modification. In this case, as described previously (see **Model Modification**, above), the approach used in this investigation occurred initially in two stages: First, following a review of the fit statistics and parameter estimates associated with the four hypothesized models, paths were added to the model guided primarily by the theoretical consequences of a path and/or insights suggested by previous research. In addition, model modification involved the use of the Lagrange multiplier (LM) tests, if suggestions provided by such tests were sensible and produced a conceptually adequate model (Dunn, Everitt & Pickles, 1993). Secondly, a path was removed from the resulting modified model if it was found to be nonsignificant when compared to α = .05.

After a review of the fit statistics and parameter estimates associated with the four hypothesized models, it was determined that minor modifications to Model 4a would significantly improve fit statistics. Moreover, the results obtained from the LM tests were also considered, however, as indicated above, only if such suggestions were sensible and produced a conceptually adequate model (Dunn, Everitt & Pickles, 1993). Following model modification, the resulting Model 4 (Final) can be seen as a minor variation of Model 4a and constitutes the final model. The steps undertaken to modify Model 4a that resulted in Model 4 (Final) are outlined immediately below.

The first modification suggested by the LM tests indicated a return path <u>back</u> from delinquency to risk behaviors, a recommendation considered not to be sensible. The second modification suggested by the LM tests recommended adding or *freeing* a path from deviant peer relationships to delinquency, a suggestion which resulted in a better model fit but that did not produce the desired fit based on the six criteria set forth previously (see **Model Fit**, above) with respect to goodness-of-fit. The third modification suggested by the LM tests on this revised model recommended freeing a path from family socioeconomic status to risk behaviors, a suggestion that also resulted in a better model fit but still did not produce the desired fit based on the six criteria for goodness-of-fit. Therefore, in addition to these modifications, a path was removed or *fixed* if it was found to be nonsignificant when compared to α = .05. Thus, the path from family socioeconomic status to parental attachment, which had not been significant in any model, and the path from parental attachment to risk behaviors, which had not been significant in any model, were both fixed to 0 in this revised model. Fixing these paths resulted in better model fit and ultimately produced a model that met all six criteria for goodness-of-fit, resulting in Model 4 (Final). In summary, the modifications to Model 4a that resulted in Model 4 (Final) consisted of freeing the following pathways: 1) deviant peer relationships to delinquency; and 2) family socioeconomic status to risk behaviors. Moreover, the modifications to Model 4a that resulted in Model 4 (Final) consisted of fixing the following pathways: 1) family socioeconomic status to parental attachment; and 2) parental attachment to risk behaviors. A description of the resulting Model 4 (Final) is presented below.

Table 6. *Summary of Model Fit for the Models*

Model	χ^2	df	χ^2/df	NFI	CFI	SRMR	RMSEA
Model 1	56.037	3	18.679	.758	.761	.076	.192
Model 1a	48.091	2	24.055	.794	.794	.067	.218
Model 2	76.544	5	15.308	.690	.698	.093	.167
Model 2a	63.881	4	15.970	.726	.732	.087	.176
Model 3	64.713	4	16.178	.722	.727	.084	.177
Model 3a	56.774	3	18.924	.758	.760	.076	.192
Model 4	68.163	5	13.633	.709	.718	.090	.161
Model 4a	60.270	4	15.068	.745	.751	.08	.172
Model 4 (Final)	4.810	3	1.603	.980	.992	.028	.035

Note: χ^2/df = chi-square/degrees of freedom (Close to 1 – Best; 0-5 – Reasonable; < 2 Preferable) NFI = Normed Fit Index (>.95 implies a good fit) CFI = Comparative Fit Index (>.95 implies a good fit) SRMR = Standardized Root Mean Squared Residual (< .08 implies a good fit) RMSEA = Root Mean-Square Error of Approximation (> 0 <= .05 – Close; = .08 – Marginal; = .10 – Poor)

Discussion of Models

In the present investigation, hypothetical models (Models, 1, 2, 3, 4 and 4 Final) that specify the relationships among parental attachment, family socioeconomic status, deviant peer relationships and youth involvement in risk behaviors and delinquency were evaluated.

Within-model alternative hypothesized causal relationships among the variables were also examined. For each of the five models, the structure coefficients and their standard errors, measuring sampling error and indicating how precisely the sample statistic estimates the population parameter (Vogt, 1999), are presented in Figure 2, along with the *within-model* alternative hypothesized causal relationships. Pathways between variables considered significant ($p < .05$) are outlined in bold. With respect to Model 4 (Final), in addition to displaying the structure coefficients and standard errors, disturbance terms, accounting for uncontrolled or unexplained variability (Vogt, 1999), are also presented.

Figure 2. Resultant Path Coefficients and Standard Errors of Exogenous and Endogenous Variable Relationships

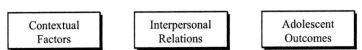

Model 1

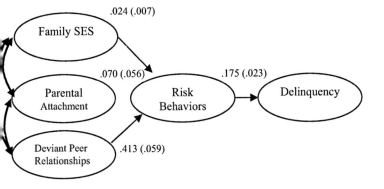

Model 1a

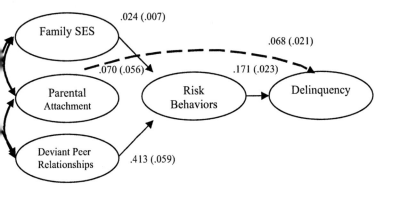

Contextual Factors	Interpersonal Relations	Adolescent Outcomes

Model 2

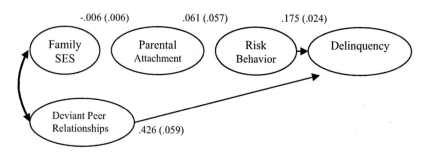

Model 2a

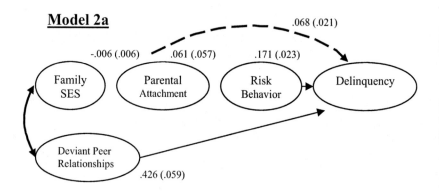

| Contextual Factors | Interpersonal Relations | Adolescent Outcomes |

Model 3

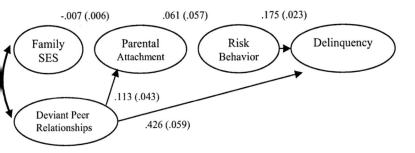

Model 3a

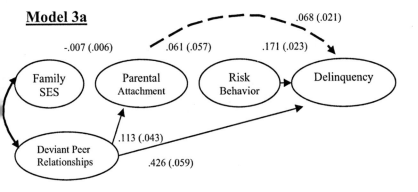

Model 4

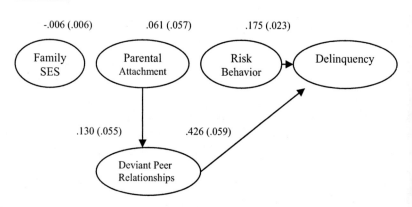

Model 4a

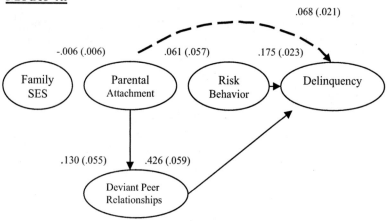

Contextual Factors	Interpersonal Relations	Adolescent Outcomes

<u>Model 4 (Final)</u>

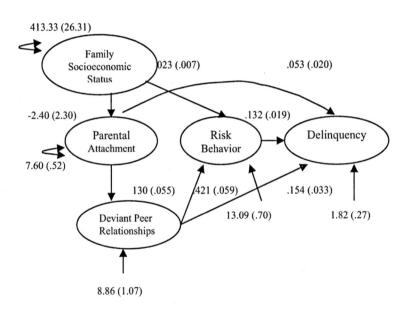

It was hypothesized that in Model 1 family socioeconomic status and parental attachment would each be directly although inversely related to risk behaviors. Moreover, it was hypothesized that deviant peer relationships would be directly related to risk behaviors. Finally, it was hypothesized that risk behaviors would be directly related to delinquency. For the most part, these hypotheses were confirmed as family socioeconomic status was significantly inversely related to risk behaviors ($p < .05$). In addition, deviant peer relationships was significantly related to risk behaviors ($p < .05$). Moreover, risk behaviors was significantly related to delinquency ($p < .05$). However, contrary to expectations, parental attachment was not significantly related to risk behaviors ($p > .05$). Moreover, as indicated above, based on the recommended criteria with respect to goodness-of-fit, Model 1 was rejected.

Model 1a, a variant of Model 1, posited an additional *alternative* hypothesized direct although inverse causal relationship between parental attachment and delinquency. This hypothesis was confirmed as parental attachment was significantly inversely related to delinquency ($p < .05$). Nevertheless, as indicated above, based on the recommended criteria with respect to goodness-of-fit, Model 1a was rejected.

Model 2 specified that family socioeconomic status would be directly related to parental attachment. This model also posited that parental attachment would be directly although inversely related to risk behaviors. Moreover, it was hypothesized that deviant peer relationships would be directly related to risk behaviors. Finally, it was hypothesized that risk behaviors would be directly related to delinquency. However, contrary to model expectations, two of these hypotheses were not supported: Family socioeconomic status was not significantly related to parental attachment ($p > .05$); and, parental attachment was not significantly related to risk behaviors ($p > .05$). On the other hand, similar to findings in Model 1, deviant peer relationships were significantly related to risk behaviors ($p < .05$) and risk behaviors were significantly related to delinquency ($p < .05$). However, as indicated above, based on the recommended criteria with respect to goodness-of-fit, Model 2 was rejected.

Model 2a, a variant of Model 2 and similar to Model 1a, in that it posited an additional *alternative* hypothesized direct although inverse causal relationship between parental attachment and delinquency. Similar to findings in Model 1a parental attachment was significantly inversely related to delinquency ($p < .05$). Nevertheless, as indicated above, based on the recommended criteria with respect to goodness-of-fit, Model 2a was rejected.

Model 3 can be seen as a modification of Model 2 that posited an additional direct path from deviant peer relationships to parental attachment. All other variable relationships in Model 3 are the same to those previously described in Model 2. Again, contrary to model expectations, two of these hypotheses were not supported: Family socioeconomic status was not significantly related to parental attachment ($p > .05$); and, parental attachment was not significantly related to risk behaviors ($p > .05$). On the other hand, similar to findings in Model 1 and Model 2, deviant peer relationships was significantly related to risk behaviors ($p < .05$) and risk behaviors was significantly related to delinquency ($p < .05$). Moreover, deviant peer relationships was significantly inversely related to parental attachment ($p < .05$). Nevertheless, as indicated above, based on the recommended criteria with respect to goodness-of-fit, Model 3 was rejected. Model 3a, a variant of Model 3 and similar to

Model 2a, in that it posited an additional *alternative* hypothesized direct causal relationship between parental attachment and delinquency. Similar to findings in Model 1a and Model 2a, parental attachment was indeed significantly inversely related to delinquency ($p < .05$). Nevertheless, as indicated above, based on the recommended criteria with respect to goodness-of-fit, Model 3a was rejected.

Model 4 can be seen as a modification of Model 3, in which the path from deviant peer relationships to parental attachment was reversed, with parental attachment posited as a cause of deviant peer relationships, rather than as a result of deviant peer relationships, as it was viewed in Model 3. As such, it was posited that parental attachment would be directly although inversely related to deviant peer relationships. All other variable relationships in Model 4 are the same as those previously described in Model 3. Again, contrary to expectations, two of these hypotheses were not supported: Family socioeconomic status was not significantly related to parental attachment ($p > .05$); and, parental attachment was not significantly related to risk behaviors ($p > .05$). On the other hand, parental attachment was again significantly inversely related to deviant peer relationships ($p < .05$). Also, similar to findings in Models 1, 2, and 3, deviant peer relationships was significantly related to risk behaviors ($p < .05$). Finally, risk behaviors were significantly related to delinquency ($p < .05$). Nevertheless, as indicated above, based on the recommended criteria with respect to goodness-of-fit, Model 4 was rejected.

Model 4a, a variant of Model 4 and similar to Model 3a in that it posited an additional *alternative* hypothesized direct although inverse causal relationship between parental attachment and delinquency. Similar to findings in Model 1a, Model 2a, and Model 3a, parental attachment was significantly inversely related to delinquency ($p < .05$). Nevertheless, as indicated above, based on the recommended criteria with respect to goodness-of-fit, Model 4a was rejected. Model 4 (Final) can be seen as a minor variation of Model 4a and constitutes the final model, with family socioeconomic status posited as being directly related to risk behaviors, albeit inversely and without the mediating variable of parental attachment, such that an increase in family socioeconomic status was related to a decrease in risk behaviors. In addition, parental attachment is no longer posited as being directly related to risk behaviors. All other variable relationships in Model 4 (Final) are similar to those described in Model 4. Consistent with expectations, family socioeconomic status was significantly inversely related to risk behaviors ($p < .05$) such that an increase in family socioeconomic status was related to a decrease in risk behaviors. In addition, parental attachment was significantly inversely related to deviant peer relationships ($p < .05$) such that an increase in parental attachment was related to a decrease in deviant peer relationships. Similar to findings in Model 1a, Model 2a, Model 3a, and Model 4a parental attachment was significantly inversely related to delinquency ($p < .05$) such that an increase in parental attachment was related to a decrease in delinquency. Moreover, similar to findings in Models 1, 2, 3, and 4 deviant peer relationships was significantly related to risk behaviors ($p < .05$) such that an increase in deviant peer relationships was related to an increase in risk behaviors. Deviant peer relationships was also significantly related to delinquency ($p < .05$) such that an increase in deviant peer relationships was related to an increase in delinquency. Finally, risk behaviors were significantly related to delinquency ($p < .05$) such that an increase in risk behaviors was related to an increase in delinquency. As indicated above, based on the recommended criteria with respect to goodness-of-fit, Model 4 (Final) was accepted.

Gender Considerations

As part of this investigation, the relationship of gender to youth involvement in risk behaviors and delinquency was also examined. Research suggests that consideration of gender differences is fundamental to an understanding of the involvement of youth in risk behaviors and delinquency (Chesney-Lind, 1986; Chesney-Lind & Shelden, 1992; Daly, 1994; Nichols, Graber, Brooks-Gunn, & Botvin, 2006; Piquero, Gover, MacDonald, & Piquero, 2005; Rhodes & Fischer, 1993; Sarigiani et al., 1999; Steffensmeier, Schwartz, Zhong, Ackerman, 2005).

The present investigation employed a multi-stage strategy to assess possible gender differences between males and females regarding their participation in risk behaviors and delinquency. The first step in this process was to determine if significant gender differences existed between males and females by examining the nature and extent of their respective involvement in such activities. (In order to partially control for the cumulative error rate associated with a relatively large number of significance tests, α was set at .01.) If significant differences were found between males and females in either risk behaviors and/or delinquent activities, the specific subscales that comprised these constructs were examined to assess whether significant gender differences (α = .01) were present. If significant gender differences were again found between the two groups as a result of examining these subscales, the final step in the process involved examining the individual items that comprised the subscales to determine if significant gender differences ($p < .01$) were again present.

Results of this examination (see **Table 7**, below) were consistent with previous findings in the literature, in that adolescent males and females participated in many of the same types of risk behaviors and delinquent activities (Chesney-Lind, 1997; Chesney-Lind & Shelden, 1992; Hartjen & Priyadarsini, 2003; Johnston et al., 2001; Moffitt, Caspi, Rutter, & Silva, 2001; Nichols, Graber, Brooks-Gunn, & Botvin, 2006; Piquero, Gover, MacDonald, & Piquero, 2005; Wallace Jr., et al., 2003). In addition, consistent with other research findings (Agnew, 2001; Elliott, 1994; Loeber & Stouthamer-Loeber, 1998; Nichols, Graber, Brooks-Gunn, & Botvin, 2006) males were found to have participated in a greater number and variety of these types of behaviors than girls. With respect to the specific types of deviant behaviors to which males and females were likely to be involved, the literature primarily speaks of males being more likely to engage in property crimes, substance use, and violent behaviors than females (Agnew, 2001; Barnow, Lucht, & Freyberger, 2005; Chesney-Lind & Shelden, 1992; Herrenkohl, et al., 2000; Loeber & Stouthamer-Loeber, 1998; Piquero, Gover, MacDonald, & Piquero, 2005; Smetana, Crean, & Daddis, 2002) with this examination finding similar results. In addition, research indicates that females are more likely than males to participate in minor crimes or status offenses including larceny theft, running away from home, truancy, and incorrigibility (Chesney-Lind, 1986; 1989; Chesney-Lind & Shelden, 1992; Morash, 1986; Naffine, 1989; Rhodes & Fischer, 1993; Siegel & Senna, 1991; Sondheimer, 2001). However, contrary to such findings, this examination found that there *were* significant differences between males and females with respect to larceny theft with males actually being *more likely* than females to have either tried to steal or to have stolen a bicycle. In addition, this examination found that there were *no* significant differences between males and females with respect to running away from home. Moreover, this examination found that there *were* significant differences between males and females with respect to incorrigibility as males were *more likely* than females to actively defy or refuse to comply with adults' requests, *more likely* to argue with adults, and *more likely* to be disobedient at school. Furthermore, this examination found that there *were n*o significant differences between males and females with respect to truancy.

Table 7. *Gender Differences in Endogenous and Exogenous Variable Relationships*

	Male *M*	Female *M*	*F*	*p*
1. Risk Behaviors	6.23 (3.94)	4.42 (3.53)	31.48	< .0001
a. SPP	3.44 (2.23)	2.69 (2.18)	15.75	< .0001
b. SCP	2.62 (2.24)	1.65 (1.98)	28.62	< .0001
c. ATOD	.12 (0.43)	.07 (0.29)	2.56	
d. EIRS	.05 (.210)	.01 (.104)		.01
2. Delinquency	1.62 (1.83)	1.03 (1.21)	19.40	< .0001
a. COV	.03 (0.19)	.00 (0.06)	4.90	< .001
b. CAPP	.70 (1.31)	.36 (0.90)	12.56	.002
c. SO	.86 (0.72)	.67 (0.67)	10.14	
d. IDPD	.03 (0.18)	.00 (0.00)	5.88	
3. Parental Attachment	6.58 (2.78)	6.67 (2.87)	.15	
a. VS	.67 (0.73)	.61 (0.71)		
b. IOC	1.05 (1.45)	1.22 (1.46)		
c. AI	4.15 (1.30)	4.21 (1.42)		
d. JLI	.71 (0.66)	.64 (0.64)		

Table 7. cont.

	Male *M*	Female *M*	*F*	*p*
4. Family SES	72.82 (19.89)	73.18 (20.80)	.04	
a. PE	3.51 (0.68)	3.57 (0.65)		
b. PO	4.35 (1.71)	4.37 (1.88)		
c. FI	3.99 (1.44)	4.06 (1.40)		
5. Deviant peers	2.43 (3.31)	1.57 (2.55)	11.35	.001

Note: SPP = School Performance Problems; SCP = School Conduct Problems; ATOD = Alcohol, Tobacco, and Other Drug Use; and EIRS = Early Involvement in Risky Sex. COV = Crimes of Violence; CAPP = Crimes Against Property and/or Person; SO = Status Offenses; and IDPD = Illicit Drug Possession and/or Distribution. VS = Virtual Supervision; IOC = Intimacy of Communication; AI = Affectional Identification; and JLI = Joint and/or Leisure Involvement. PE = Parental Education; PO = Parental Occupation; and FI = Family Income.

Table 8. *Gender Differences in Endogenous and Exogenous Variable Relationships By Item*

1) Risk Behaviors

School Performance Problems

Q: Have you ever had to repeat a grade because you failed?

	Male	Female	χ^2	*p*
Yes	48 (19%)	28 (10%)	7.61	.01
No	212	248		

Q: Fails to complete assignments.

	Male	Female	χ^2	*p*
Yes	166 (64%)	136 (49%)	11.56	.001
No	94	140		

Q: Lacks interest in schoolwork.

	Male	Female	χ^2	*p*
Yes	126 (51%)	82 (30%)	23.56	.0001
No	120	189		

Table 8.cont.

		School Performance Problems cont.		

Q: Poor schoolwork.

	Male	Female	χ^2	p
Yes	131 (54%)	112 (41%)	8.57	.003
No	112	161		

		School Conduct Problems		

Q: How often have you been send to school guidance counselor or school psychologist?

	Male	Female	χ^2	p
Yes	86 (33%)	62 (23%)	7.55	.006
No	174	214		

Q: Have you ever been suspended from school?

	Male	Female	χ^2	p
Yes	148 (57%)	90 (33%)	32.06	<.0001
No	112	186		

Q: Actively defies or refuses to comply with adults' requests.

	Male	Female	χ^2	p
Yes	100 (57%)	71 (33%)	12.17	<.001
No	146	200		

Q: Argues with adults.

	Male	Female	χ^2	p
Yes	99 (40%)	75 (28%)	9.123	.003
No	147	196		

Q: Disobedient at school.

	Male	Female	χ^2	p
Yes	101 (42%)	77 (28%)	10.15	.001
No	142	196		

Table 8. cont.				
1) Risk Behaviors cont.				
School Conduct Problems cont.				
Q: Gets in many fights.				
	Male	Female	χ^2	*p*
Yes	54 (22%)	25 (9%)	17.10	<.0001
No	188	248		
Early involvement in risky sex				
Q: Have you ever had sexual activity with someone more than kissing or hugging?				
	Male	Female	χ^2	*p*
Yes	12 (5%)	3 (1%)	6.09	.01
No	248	272		
2) Delinquency				
Crimes against property/person				
Q: Have you ever damaged or destroyed property that did not belong to you, for example, spray paint buildings, smash car windows, or slash tires?				
	Male	Female	χ^2	*p*
Yes	45 (17%)	21 (8%)	11.66	.001
No	215	255		
Q: Have you ever stole or tried to steal a bicycle?				
	Male	Female	χ^2	*p*
Yes	19 (7%)	6 (2%)	7.94	.005
No	241	270		
Q: Have you ever seriously hurt someone physically on purpose?				
	Male	Female	χ^2	*p*
Yes	17 (7%)	5 (2%)	7.60	.006
No	243	271		

Table 8. cont.

2) Delinquency cont.

Crimes against property/person cont.

Q: Have you ever set things or property on fire?

	Male	Female	χ^2	p
Yes	19 (7%)	4 (1%)	11.18	.001
No	241	272		

Status offenses

Q: Have your parents ever been asked to come to school because you missed school or misbehaved?

	Male	Female	χ^2	p
Yes	130 (50%)	85 (31%)	20.55	<.0001
No	130	191		

3) Deviant peer relationships

Association with deviant peers

Q: Have any of your close friends ever been expelled from school?

	Male	Female	χ^2	p
Yes	136 (53%)	80 (30%)	28.01	<.0001
No	122	187		

Q: How many of your close friends have ever stolen to tried to steal a bicycle?

	Male	Female	χ^2	p
Yes	64 (27%)	39 (15%)	10.29	.001
No	174	218		

Q: How many of your close friends have ever set things or property on fire?

	Male	Female	χ^2	p
Yes	40 (17%)	20 (8%)	9.56	.002
No	197	237		

Table 8. cont.				
4) Deviant peer relationships cont.				
Association with deviant peers cont.				
Q: Hangs around with others who get in trouble.				
	Male	Female	χ^2	p
Yes	110 (45%)	71 (26%)	20.94	<.0001
No	133	202		

Finally, Model 4 (Final) was separately fit in males and females, with all free parameters constrained to be equal in the two samples. However, this model was rejected because the χ^2 value was high (80.6), the *NFI* and *CFI* values were less than .95 (.65 and .69), and the *SRMR* value was greater than .08 (.17), indicating poor fit of the model. Constraints were then relaxed to allow for unequal disturbance terms. This model fit the data quite well, as the χ^2 value and relative chi-square statistic were both low (17.183 and 1.43), the *NFI* value was slightly less than .95 (.93), the *CFI* value was greater than .95 (.98), the *SRMR* value was less than .08 (.05), and the *RMSEA* value was less than .05 (.03). Such a model indicates that the disturbance terms and thus the R^2 associated with each structural equation differ for males and females. (The structure coefficients and disturbance terms for this model can be found in **Table 9**, below.) Examination of the R^2 values suggests that the explanatory power of the model is better for females than males (see **Table 9**, below). Such results are similar to previous research findings which suggest that social control theory may be a better predictor of female than male delinquency (Krohn & Massey, 1980; Rosenbaum, 1987; Siegal & Senna, 1991; Walters, 1992).

Table 9. *Structure Coefficients and Disturbance Terms for Males and Females*

Path	Structure Coefficients	Disturbance Terms		R^2	
		Males	Females	Males	Females
PA → AWDP	.126 (.045)				
		11.03 (.99)	6.39 (.56)	.010	.020
SES → RB	.024 (.008)				
AWDP → RB	.382 (.053)				
		13.82 (1.24)	11.40 (1.00)	.118	.095
PA → DQ	.071 (.020)				
AWDP → DQ	.139 (.021)				
RB → DQ	.111 (.016)				
		2.55 (.23)	1.10 (.10)	.191	.278

Note: SES = Socioeconomic Status; PA = Parental Attachment; AWDP = Associations with Deviant Peers; RB = Risk Behaviors; and DQ = Delinquency. The standard errors for both the Structure Coefficients and Disturbance Terms are in parenthesis.

Table 10. *Simple Correlations between Study Variables for Males and Females*

Index Score	SES	PA	AWDP	RB	DQ
Males above the diagonal; Females below the diagonal					
SES		-.012	.080	.138	.100
PA	-.071		.106	.065	.072
AWDP	.069	.166		.334	.421
RB	.162	.106	.278		.434
DQ	.068	.298	.356	.360	
Males					
M	72.82	6.58	2.43	6.23	1.62
SD	19.89	2.78	3.31	3.94	1.83
Possible Range	3-116	0-23	0-20	0-32	0-25
Females					
M	73.18	6.67	1.57	4.42	1.03
SD	20.80	2.87	2.55	3.53	1.21
Possible Range	3-116	0-23	0-20	0-32	0-25

Note: SES = Socioeconomic Status; PA = Parental Attachment; AWDP = Associations with Deviant Peers; RB = Risk Behaviors; and DQ = Delinquency. In addition, M = Mean; and SD = Standard Deviation.

CHAPTER 5

Discussion and Conclusions

In the present investigation, a cross-sectional design and a structural equation modeling statistical approach were used to evaluate the viability of four conceptual models in explaining the relationships among parental attachment, family socioeconomic status, deviant peer relationships and youth involvement in risk behaviors and delinquency. Although specific relationship pathways within the four hypothetical models were found to be significant, the hypothesized models themselves failed to fit the data. Of particular note was the finding across all four models that family socioeconomic status was not significantly related to parental attachment and parental attachment was not significantly related to risk behaviors although recent findings had suggested otherwise (Bellair & Roscigno, 2000; Fergusson, Swain-Campbell, & Horwood, 2004; LeBlanc, 1992; Sampson & Laub, 1995). Such results may be related to the make-up of this study's sample, which was comprised solely of African American youth while previous research samples were comprised of youth from various ethnocultural groups, which may suggest differential relationships among these variables with respect to African American youth.

With respect to Model 4 Final, this model fit the data quite well as the relationship pathways between family socioeconomic status and parental attachment, as well as parental attachment and risk behaviors were removed. [For a more detailed discussion of such modifications and the resulting Model 4 (Final) see the section entitled Model

Modification above.] The results of Model 4 (Final) suggest that consistent with previous findings in the literature (Cernkovich & Giordano, 1987; Jensen & Rojek, 1992; Kempf, 1993; Rosenbaum, 1989; Sampson & Laub, 1995; Stern & Smith, 1995) the dimension of attachment, specifically parental attachment, as posited in Hirschi's social control theory (1969), was significantly related to youth participation in delinquent activities. These findings suggest that higher parental attachment is related to decreased youth participation in delinquency while lower parental attachment is related to increased participation.

Parental attachment was not significantly related to youth participation in risk behaviors, a result that was contrary to hypothesized model expectations and previous research findings (Rankin & Kern, 1994). However, higher parental attachment was significantly related to decreased youth involvement in deviant peer relationships, a finding that is consistent with Hirschi's own results following an evaluation of social control theory in his seminal work *Causes of Delinquency*, in particular, and other research findings (Dunst & Trivette, 1994; Hawkins et al., 1992; Henry, 2001; Howard et al., 1999; Kandel & Andrews, 1987; Rutter 1987, 1993; Pardini, Loeber, & Stouthamer-Loeber, 2005; Rankin & Kern, 1994; Stanton et al., 2002; Thornton et al., 2000; Warr, 1993b, 2005).

Higher youth involvement in deviant peer relationships was significantly related to subsequent participation in both risk behaviors and delinquency. Such findings are consistent with those of Hirschi (1969), who found in his evaluation of social control theory that youth with delinquent friends were themselves more likely to become delinquent. However, Hirschi admitted that social control theory, itself, "...underestimated the importance of delinquent friends; [as]

it overestimated the significance of involvement in conventional activities" (Hirschi, 1969, p. 230). Such results are also consistent with prior research findings, which have suggested for many years and across various studies, that youth who are involved in deviant peer relationships are likely to participate in deviant activities (Brown, Eicher, & Petrie, 1986; Chung & Steinberg, 2006; Elliott, Huizinga, & Ageton, 1985; Heinze, Toro, & Urberg, 2004; Pardini, Loeber, & Stouthamer-Loeber, 2005; Shaw & McKay, 1931; Warr, 2002, 2005).

As hypothesized, family socioeconomic status was significantly related to youth participation in risk behaviors. However, contrary to model expectations, this did not occur indirectly through the mediating variable of parental attachment, but instead was a direct inverse relationship. As such, these findings suggest that higher family socioeconomic status is related to decreased youth participation in risk behaviors while lower family socioeconomic status is related to increased youth participation in risk behaviors. These findings were both expected and unexpected, in that, Bellair & Roscigno (2000); Fergusson, Swain-Campbell, & Horwood (2004); and Sampson & Laub (1995) found that family socioeconomic status was related to youth participation in risk behaviors, but through the mediating variable of parental attachment. Nevertheless, the results of this examination suggest that a direct inverse relationship exists between the two. However, as previously suggested (see **Family Socioeconomic Status**, above), conclusions drawn from previous research results must be tempered because the research evidence is still relatively sparse, and as such, the results of this study build upon the growing but limited work that examines the nature of such relationships (Bellair & Roscigno, 2000; Fergusson, Swain-Campbell, & Horwood,

2004; LeBlanc, 1992; Sampson & Laub, 1995; Wadsworth, 2000).

With respect to parental attachment, the findings of this investigation contribute to the body of knowledge regarding the primacy of parents (caregivers) as key socializing agents and a frontline defense against youth participation in deviant behaviors. Moreover, the results of the investigation correspond with previous findings regarding the role that risk and protective factors play in the development of deviant behaviors among youth. Research suggests that protective factors enhance internal strengths and foster resilience in adolescents, which moderates the impact of risks by reducing or offsetting vulnerabilities and environmental hazards, thereby enabling individuals to cope with adversity (Davis, 1999; Masten & Coatsworth, 1998; Mrazek & Haggerty, 1994; O'Leary, 1998). Prominent protective factors identified in studies comparing non-deviant and deviant individuals in poor urban neighborhoods include close attachment to parents, the presence of positive adult role models, and associations with non-deviant peers (Dunst & Trivette, 1994; Hawkins et al., 1992; Howard et al., 1999; Rutter 1987, 1993; Thornton et al., 2000; Weaver & Prelow, 2005). The results of this investigation reaffirm such findings as they suggest that high parental attachment leads to decreased youth involvement in deviant peer relationships and decreased participation in delinquent activities. In addition, these results reaffirm the strong influence of deviant peer relationships as they suggest that involvement with deviant peers leads to increased participation in both risk behaviors and delinquency. Finally, similar to previous research findings (Gottfredson, 2001; Jessor, 1998; Loeber & Stouthamer-Loeber, 1987), higher youth participation in risk behaviors was related to higher participation in delinquency.

These results suggest that youth participation in risk behaviors is a precursor for subsequent participation in more serious delinquent activities.

With respect to African American youth and their families who live in socially and economically disadvantaged urban environments, in particular, the findings of this investigation suggest that increased parental attachment decreases youth involvement in delinquent activities and deviant peer relationships and that such attachments may overcome some of the negative influences associated with living in such environments.

Moreover, the present investigation's findings may provide additional insight into the results of other research studies which have suggested for many years that despite the comparatively high prevalence of numerous social problems in poor urban neighborhoods, most individuals who live in such high-risk environments emerge relatively problem-free (Garmezy, 1985; Hawkins et al., 1992; Howard et al., 1999; Mrazek & Haggerty, 1994) as such individuals may have had strong parental attachments, which appear to mitigate the negative influences associated with living in disadvantaged urban communities.

Gender Considerations

Previous research findings suggest that Hirschi's social control theory (1969) is an appropriate theoretical model in explaining female delinquency (Hindelang, 1973; Jensen & Eve, 1976; Walters, 1992; Warren, 1983), with some research results even suggesting that social control theory may be a better predictor of female than male delinquency (Krohn & Massey, 1980; Rosenbaum, 1987; Siegal & Senna, 1991; Walters, 1992). Moreover, in studies comparing the explanatory power of Hirschi's social control theory (1969) versus social strain theory (Merton, 1957), in particular, previous research findings have been more supportive of social control theory (Hepburn, 1976; Stack, 1982; Thornberry et al., 1985; Walters, 1992). Furthermore, serious concerns have been raised regarding the explanatory power of social strain theory in general (Lilly, Cullen, & Ball, 1989; Empey, 1982; Kornhhauser, 1978; Pfohl, 1985; Vold & Bernard, 1986) and specifically with respect to female crime and delinquency (Chesney-Lind & Shelden, 1992; Morris, 1987). These concerns have to do with the basic tenets of strain theory which posit that strain arises in individuals when the culturally defined success goals of society are not legitimately obtainable resulting in some individuals participating in illegitimate means to obtain sought after goals (Chesney-Lind & Shelden, 1992; Lilly, Cullen, & Ball, 1989; Siegal & Senna, 1991). Morris (1987) suggest that if this were the case, then women, who through various forms of discrimination have not been afforded many of the same opportunities as men, should participate in more delinquent acts than men. Because this has not been found to be the case, the explanatory power of the theory, with respect to female participation in crime and delinquency, has been seriously undermined (Chesney-Lind & Shelden, 1992; Morris, 1987). Moreover, strain resulting from increased exposure to contemporary life conditions may not manifest into greater involvement in violent or deviant activities (Steffensmeier, Schwartz, Zhong, & Ackerman, 2005), as research suggest that females under stress are more likely than males to engage in negative *internalizing* behaviors (Achenbach, 1982; Barber et al., 1994; Leadbeater, Blatt, & Quinlan, 1995; Hagan & Foster, 2003; Zahn-Waxler, 1993; Wagner & Compas, 1990).

The results of the present investigation suggest that males and females participate in many of the same types of risk behaviors and delinquent activities. As such, the results of this study are similar to previous research findings suggesting that males and females participate in many of the same types of deviant behaviors (Chesney-Lind, 1997; Chesney-Lind & Shelden, 1992; Hartjen & Priyadarsini, 2003; Johnston et al., 2001; Moffitt, Caspi, Rutter, & Silva, 2001; Nichols, Graber, Brooks-Gunn, & Botvin, 2006; Piquero, Gover, MacDonald, & Piquero, 2005; Wallace Jr., et al., 2003), with males typically participating in such acts in greater variety and more frequently than females (Agnew, 2001; Barnow, Lucht, & Freyberger, 2005; Chesney-Lind & Shelden, 1992; Elliott, 1994; Loeber & Stouthamer-Loeber, 1998; Nichols, Graber, Brooks-Gunn, & Botvin, 2006; Piquero, Gover, MacDonald, & Piquero, 2005).

An alternative interpretation of the above findings may lie in the results obtained from research on stress. Numerous studies related to this topic suggest that, when under stress, males are more likely than females to engage in negative *externalizing* behaviors (e.g., aggression, conduct problems, delinquency), whereas females are more likely to engage in negative *internalizing* behaviors (e.g., anxiety, sadness, depression) (Achenbach, 1982; Barber et al., 1994; Leadbeater, Blatt, & Quinlan, 1995; Hagan & Foster, 2003; Henggeler, 1989; Rutter & Garmezy, 1983; Zahn-Waxler, 1993; Wagner & Compas, 1990). As the assessment measures utilized in the present investigation focused more on assessing external behavior than internal signs of such behavior, it is plausible that this resulted in the base rates for males, with respect to stress-related behavior, being higher than for females, potentially influencing the interpretation of results and the conclusions drawn from the investigation.

Contrary to previous findings from arrest data (Chesney-Lind, 1986, 1989, 1997; Chesney-Lind & Shelden, 1992; Morash, 1986; Naffine, 1989; Rhodes & Fischer, 1993; Siegel & Senna, 1991), the results of the present investigation suggest that females are less likely than males to be involved in minor crimes or status offenses, specifically with respect to larceny theft, and truancy. Moreover, this investigation found no significant differences between males and females with respect to running away from home. A plausible explanation for such discrepant findings may lie in the fact that the present investigation utilized *self-report* data as opposed to *arrest data* to determine the extent of male and female participation in such activities. Reviews of both sources of data reveal that in self-report surveys males and females are likely to report similar rates of participation in minor crimes or status offenses while reviews of arrest data indicate that females participate in these activities more frequently than males (Canter, 1982; Chesney-Lind, 1986, 1989, 1997; Chesney-Lind & Shelden, 1992; Steffensmeier & Steffensmeier, 1980). The results of this investigation are similar to research findings in which self-report data were utilized to assess male and female involvement in minor crimes or status offenses.

Finally, results of the present investigation extend previous research findings regarding male and female participation in deviant behaviors by providing item-by-item comparisons of commonly and less commonly cited findings regarding the nature and extent of involvement in specific types of risk behaviors and delinquent activities (see **Table 9**, above). Moreover, the results obtained from Model 4 Final indicate that the disturbance terms and thus the R^2 associated with each structural equation differ for males and females. (The structure coefficients and disturbance terms for this model can be found in **Table 9**, above.) Examination of the R^2 values suggests that the explanatory power of the model is better for females than males (see **Table 9**, above). Such results are similar to previous research findings which suggest that social control theory may be a better predictor of female than male delinquency (Krohn & Massey, 1980; Rosenbaum, 1987; Siegal & Senna, 1991; Walters, 1992).

Age Considerations

Although it was initially anticipated that age would be examined to assess its relationship to parental attachment and youth deviance, as previous research (Krohn & Massey, 1980; LaGrange & White, 1985; Seydlitz, 1993) had indicated that such relationships vary with respect to age, following a thorough review and analysis of the dataset, it was determined that such an examination would be unproductive as the age ranges of the participants showed little variability.

Urban African American Youth At-Risk

As outlined in the introduction, youth participation in risk behaviors and delinquency are both serious social problems in the United States, with the number of adolescents participating in such behaviors continuing to rise, while the age at which they become involved in such activities continues to fall (Farrington et al., 2002; Miller, Brehm, & Whitehouse, 1998; Smith & Stern, 1997; Thornton et al., 2000). For decades, empirical research has consistently demonstrated that the early involvement of youth in risk behaviors and delinquency places them in jeopardy of progressing along deviant pathways that, if left unchecked, are likely to continue into adulthood and have life-long detrimental consequences for their health and well-being (Anglin & Speckart, 1988; Chaiken & Chaiken, 1982, 1990; Gottfredson, 2001; Grunbaum et al., 2002; Ingoldsby & Shaw, 2002; Jessor, 1998; Newcomb, Maddahian, & Bentler, 1986). This is a particularly serious problem for African American youth who reside in America's cities as many of them live in socially and physically disordered communities characterized by high rates of crime, violence, drug trafficking (selling and delivering), and urban blight, with graffiti, trash, junk-filled vacant lots, abandoned cars, and boarded-up or abandoned buildings being prominent features of many of their neighborhoods (Gorham, 1992; O'Donnell et al., 2001; Skogan, 1990; Wilson, 1996). Moreover, many of these youth are represented among the chronically poor, are disproportionately exposed to stressful life conditions, and frequently witness and eventually become involved in illegal activities, such as drug use and drug trafficking (Bell & Jenkins, 1993; Duncan & Yeung, 1995; Fagan, 1993; Garbarino et al., 1991; Grant et al., 2000; Huston, McLoyd, & Coll, 1994; Jessor, 1993; McLeod & Shanahan, 1993). Studies have shown that exposure to these types of adverse social and environmental conditions may result in psychological and behavioral problems, including depression, hopelessness, substance abuse, delinquency, and violent behavior (Freudenberg et al., 1999; Garbarino, 1995a, 1995b; Pickrel et al., 1997).

The results of this investigation clearly suggest that regardless of the fact that the participants in this investigation reside in socially and economically disadvantaged urban communities in Baltimore City, increased parental attachment and higher family socioeconomic status may help mitigate some of the negative influences associated with living in such environments. Youth who live in such communities who are strongly attached to their parents are less likely to participate in delinquent activities and become involved in deviant peer relationships. Moreover, higher family socioeconomic status appears to be related to reduced youth participation in risk behaviors. Those families that lack strong parent and child attachments and have relatively low family socioeconomic statuses may be adversely impacted by individual, social, and community factors that leave them at a disadvantage.

CHAPTER 6

Social and Policy Recommendations

The findings of this study contribute to the body of knowledge within sociological theory regarding the importance of both macro and micro level factors in promoting and/or restraining individual behavior. More specifically, with respect to sociological explanations of crime and deviance, the results of this study reaffirm the primacy of parents (caregivers) as key socializing agents and a frontline defense against youth deviance. These findings suggest that youth who maintain strong parental attachments are less likely to be involved with deviant peers and participate in delinquent activities. In addition, these results reaffirm the strong influence of deviant peers as youth involvement in deviant peer relationships was related to increased youth participation in both risk behaviors and delinquency. With respect to stratification theory, the results of this study suggest that macro-level factors are related to youth deviance as higher family socioeconomic status was related to decreased youth participation in risk behaviors. Overall, the findings from this study suggest that early preventive strategies aimed at reducing problem behaviors among youth that intervene either at the micro-level to impact parental attachment and deviant peer relationships or at the macro-level to impact family socioeconomic status will not solve the problem of youth participation in risk behaviors and delinquency. Instead, effective interventions at both levels would be required (Fergusson, Swain-Campbell, & Horwood, 2004).

With respect to micro-level factors, in general, advocates of social control theory recommend that social and policy recommendations involve protecting and insulating youth from those negative factors that may influence their participation in deviant activities (Lanier & Henry, 1998). Such recommendations focus on the forging of strong bonds between youth and conventional social institutions, including the family, through intensive socialization in traditional and conventional belief systems (Empey, 1982; Lanier & Henry, 1998; Lilly, Cullen, & Ball, 1989). The primary focus of such prevention policies would be to strengthen the bonds between parent and child by promoting positive parent-child interactions and encouraging youth involvement in school-related activities (Henry, 2001; Lanier & Henry, 1998; Lilly, Cullen, & Ball, 1989; Morton & Ewald, 1987).

The findings of the present investigation may assist in the design, development, and/or enhancement of early preventive intervention strategies aimed at reducing problem behaviors and improving parent-child interactions among youth and their families, particularly among African American youth and their families living in socially and economically disadvantaged urban communities. These results suggest that such strategies may involve strengthening the bonds between parent and child, possibly through the development of, and utilization of, after-school programs and family-focused preventive intervention programs. Previous research has consistently demonstrated that after-school programs that promote attachment or bonding to prosocial activities and people, that strengthen and nurture the familial bond between parent and child, and that are conducted under safe circumstances help to mitigate the impact of negative social environments (Freedman, 1993; Katz, 1997; McLaughlin et al., 1994). Similarly, family-focused programs targeting high-risk youth that seek to improve parent-child interactions by strengthening the bonds between parent and child are likely to decrease problem behaviors among youth, reduce associations with deviant peers, and improve youth self-concept and academic achievement (Brounstein et al., 2001a, 2001b; Hawkins et al., 1992; Henry, 2001; Rutter 1987, 1993; US DHHS, 2001; Volk et al., 1989; Webster-Stratton & Taylor, 2001; Yearwood et al., 2002).

Intervention efforts that only address risk factors at the individual or family level are likely to be less effective than comprehensive efforts, inasmuch as they may not fully take into account the complex multivariate relationships among adolescent problem behaviors. Given the results of the present investigation, which suggest that lower family socioeconomic status is related to increased youth participation in risk behaviors it is also important to address the macro-level factors underlying socially-related dynamics that may have an indirect impact on youth participation in problematic activities (Sampson & Laub, 1995).

Extant macro-level factors, including low-wages, joblessness, and poverty in socially and economically disadvantaged urban communities, are related to recent changes in the structure of American society that have resulted from deindustrialization, deconcentration, and the expansion of people and industry into the highly integrated global marketplace (Jargowsky, 1997; Piven & Cloward, 1997; Ranney, 1999; Wilson, 1996). These social conditions have made it more difficult for blue-collar and low-skilled workers throughout America, particularly in urban communities, to obtain gainful employment, a livable wage, and escape from poverty (Jennings, 1999). A dwindling employment base for residents of such communities has also led to fewer legitimate occupational opportunities for youth who live in these environments (Jargowski & Bane, 1991; Johnson et al., 1990; Peterson & Harrell, 1992; Wilson, 1987,

1996). (For a more detailed statement regarding the social processes that led to these conditions see Appendix A).

As a result of the above circumstances, many of these youth frequently witness and eventually become involved in illegal activities, such as drug use, drug trafficking, and in the attendant violence that characterizes such activities (Bell & Jenkins, 1993; Fagan, 1993; Garbarino et al., 1991). Although these adaptations have their immediate economic rewards, they clearly represent serious problem behaviors that not only run counter to the prohibitions and expectations of the larger society but in the end lead to further degradation of the individual and the community (Kopstein & Roth, 1990; Nurco et al., 1994, 1997a, 1997b; Okundaye, 2004).

Many of the macro-level problems plaguing America's urban communities can be addressed through both universal and targeted government policy initiatives that are designed to promote education, provide job retraining, and increase the minimum wage (Fergusson, Swain-Campbell, & Norwood, 2004; Jargowsky, 1997; Wilson, 1996). However, as suggested by Wilson (1987, 1996, 1999), when such initiatives are tailored to address the needs of one segment of the population over another they are invariably doomed to fail. Thus, it would be important to adopt both universal and targeted policy initiatives designed to appeal to broad coalitions of people and having the potential to reduce those macro-level factors in urban communities that indirectly impact on the participation of youth in deviant activities.

Study Limitations

The present investigation has several limitations. First, although Hirschi's social control theory was the conceptual framework utilized and is one of the most widely used theoretical approaches with respect to youth deviance (Greenberg, 1999; Jensen & Rojek, 1992; Kempf, 1993; Lanier & Henry, 1998; Siegal & Senna, 1991), one cannot entirely rule out the explanatory power of alternative theoretical approaches or the interconnectedness of competing theories (Shoemaker, 1984). Instead, it is important to recognize both the strengths and weaknesses of a particular theoretical approach when attempting to explain such phenomena and be mindful of the totality of these considerations when interpreting results and drawing conclusions. As with all theoretical approaches that address such issues, social control theory is limited in its explanatory power with respect to youth deviance (Lilly, Cullen, & Ball, 1989; Shoemaker, 1984) but is similar to other approaches in that it is capable of providing insight into the nature of the relationships between risk and protective factors and youth participation in risk behaviors and delinquent activities.

Second, as with all such studies, the present investigation is limited in terms of the generalizability of its findings. Inasmuch as the present investigation utilized existing data drawn from a sample of urban African American male and female middle school students from similar socioeconomic backgrounds, the generalizability of study findings is principally limited to youth who are similar in terms of urban residence, race, school grade, and family socioeconomic status. Moreover, because the reliability of the parental attachment index (= .54) was lower than that generally recommended in the literature (e.g., above .70; Vogt, 1999), the present study findings with respect to this measure must be viewed with some caution. [The relatively low internal consistency of this measure may have adversely impacted its relationship to family socioeconomic status and reduced its potential predictive power with respect to youth participation in risk behaviors. However, its lower reliability may not have reduced its correlation with deviant peer relationships and delinquency to the extent that it was no longer significant. These latter findings are consistent with Hirschi's own results and other research findings (Cernkovich & Giordano, 1987; Hawkins et al., 1992; Howard et al., 1999; Rutter 1987, 1993; Rankin & Kern, 1994; Rosenbaum, 1989; Stern & Smith, 1995).] In addition, the use of a cross-sectional design may limit the generalizability of research findings as the interpretation of results and study conclusions attempt to make causal statements, which are based on observations that occur over time, while the data that was utilized was based on observations that occurred at a particular point in time (Cohen et al., 2000). However, as the original intent of the study from which this investigation's data was drawn was for an after-school program evaluation (see **Sample Characteristics**, above) with one school serving as the experimental and the other as the comparison site, longitudinal information collected from one school site may have been unduly influenced by the intervention services provided to youth participating in the program.

Third, considering that parenting is a complex interactive process between parent and child (Chase-Lansdale & Pittman, 2002) and parental attachment is but one aspect of this larger process, the policy recommendations from this study with respect to parenting, in general, are correspondingly limited. However, consistent with the fact that this and other research has indicated that youth who maintain strong parental attachments are less likely to be involved with deviant peers and participate in deviant activities (Cernkovich & Giordano, 1987; Jensen & Rojek, 1992; Kempf, 1993; Rankin & Kern,

1994; Rosenbaum, 1989; Sampson & Laub, 1995; Stern & Smith, 1995) recommendations with respect to prevention and remediation of deviant behaviors have revolved around the facilitation of such parent-child interconnections. Preventive interventions that are family focused and school-based and that promote family bonding through interactive activities, including cooperative learning, group communication, field trips, and the provision of family support services, have consistently been found to strengthen the bonds between parent and child, reduce associations with deviant peers, and decrease youth participation in deviant behaviors (Brounstein et al., 2001a, 2001b; Thornton et al., 2000; US DHHS, 2001).   Fourthly, as noted above under gender considerations, caution should be exercised regarding the generalizability of study results for two distinct reasons. First, with respect to the participation of females in risk behaviors and delinquent activities, the base rates for females were lower than for males potentially influencing the interpretation of results and the conclusions drawn from these comparisons. Second, as the findings from stress research suggest, when males are under stress they appear to be more likely than females to engage in negative *externalizing* behaviors (e.g., aggression, conduct problems, delinquency), while females are more likely than males to engage in negative *internalizing* behaviors (e.g., anxiety, sadness, depression) (Achenbach, 1982; Barber et al., 1994; Leadbeater, Blatt, & Quinlan, 1995; Hagan & Foster, 2003; Henggeler, 1989; Rutter and Garmezy, 1983; Zahn-Waxler, 1993; Wagner & Compas, 1990). Because the assessment measures utilized in the present investigation focused more on assessing external behavior than internal signs of such behavior, it is plausible that this resulted in the base rates for males, with respect to stress-related behavior, being higher than for females, potentially influencing the interpretation of results and the conclusions drawn from the investigation.

Finally, as mentioned earlier (see **Theoretical Critiques of Hirschi's Social Control Theory**, above) advocates of labeling theory and also scholars within the field of critical criminology posit that differential treatment and surveillance techniques by social control agents (e.g., teachers, police, etc.) of poor, disadvantaged, and minority group members results in them being disproportionately labeled as deviants (Adams, Robertson, Gray-Ray, & Ray, 2003). This negative stigmatization leads to closer scrutiny and monitoring of their behavior by such agents and members of the larger society increasing the probability that they will be identified as miscreants (Lilly, Cullen, & Ball, 1989; Tittle, 1980, 1983). Moreover, their own internalization of such negative beliefs increases the likelihood that they will participate in deviant activities in the future (Tittle, 1980, 1983). This study, however, does not focus its attention on the nature of this labeling process, how members of such groups may be inordinately monitored and identified as deviants, and the potential negative ramifications that may occur as a result but instead focuses primarily on the role that risk and protective factors play in the involvement of youth in risk behaviors and delinquent activities.

Future Directions

As indicated earlier, a limited amount of research has focused on the underlying etiological factors associated with the participation of urban African American youth in risk behaviors and delinquent activities. The involvement of African American youth in such activities is a serious problem in American society inasmuch as it has been shown that they are more likely than White youth to drop out of school, to be involved in aggressive and violent acts, and to be victims of violent crime (Fraser, Galinsky, & Richman, 1999; Richman & Bowen, 1997; Myers & Taylor, 1998). Although the results of the present investigation contribute to the existing literature, suggesting that increased parental attachment decreases African American youth involvement in deviant peer relationships and delinquent activities, additional corroborating evidence is still needed to reaffirm such findings.

With respect to gender considerations, although the results of the present investigation contribute to the existing body of research on gender differences with respect to youth participation in deviant activities, the nature and etiology of these differences are still not fully understood, particularly among African American youth (Juon, Doherty, & Ensminger, 2006). Because of this, further investigations of the differentiating influences associated with the participation of African American female and male youth in deviant behaviors are clearly warranted.

Finally, empirical evidence has consistently demonstrated that the early involvement of youth in risk behaviors places them in jeopardy of progressing along deviant pathways that, if left unchecked, are likely to continue into adulthood and have life-long detrimental consequences for their health and well-being. Although the results of this investigation suggest that higher family socioeconomic status may reduce the involvement of youth in such activities, little research has focused on the nature of such a relationship, and present conclusions must be tempered because the of paucity of research evidence bearing on this issue. Thus, additional research aimed at elucidating the situational dynamics underlying the relationship between socioeconomic status and youth participation in risk behaviors appear warranted.

The Recent Decline of America's Cities

During the past 30 years, researchers have documented the disproportionately high rates of poverty, unemployment, crime, illicit substance abuse, illegitimate births, sexually-transmitted diseases, HIV infection, and other indicators of social disorganization that are becoming increasingly concentrated in America's cities (Jargowsky, 1997; Kasarda, 1992; Massey & Denton, 1993; O'Donnell et al., 2001, 2002; Wilson, 1987, 1996). Many of these problems are related to the seemingly innocuous and continuous movement of people from city to suburb, which initially occurred in haste at the end of World War II, and continues to the present day. Although the origins of the suburbanization of America commenced much earlier in the century, as a result of the widespread availability and use of the automobile, the enactment of legislative policies that provided low-interest loans to returning veterans and that funded massive highway construction projects across the country following World War II were the major catalysts responsible for population, demography, and landscape changes that have shaped modern American society (Karp, Stone, & Yoels, 1991; Massey & Denton, 1993).

The Move to the Suburbs

During the late 1940s and early 1950s, suburban living became attractive to many young couples as it offered them the best of both worlds, easy access to work, shopping, and entertainment facilities, outlets principally located in the cities, while simultaneously providing them with the ability to escape from the unseemly or less desirable aspects of city life by returning to their homes in the suburbs (Fischer, 1984; Karp, Stone & Yoels, 1991). Eventually, however, even those facilities and amenities that were predominate and unique to the city made their way into the suburbs as developers purchased large tracts of land in suburban locales and developed them into commercial shopping centers and entertainment facilities (Fischer, 1984; Karp, Stone & Yoels, 1991). More importantly, however, the movement of people from city to suburb was fueled by suburban home ownership, as government tax incentives and low-interest loans to returning veterans made it easier and cheaper for people to buy homes in suburban locales as opposed to cities (Massey & Denton, 1993). In addition, government funding of massive highway construction projects across the country enabled people to easily commute back and forth from suburb to city (Fischer, 1984; Karp, Stone, & Yoels, 1991). As more and more people moved from city to suburb, suburban home ownership came to viewed as the embodiment of the American Dream, that is, a clear sign of upward mobility and increased social stature, further fueling the movement of people from city to suburb (Karp, Stone, & Yoels, 1991). Thus, with more commercial and entertainment outlets available in the suburbs, government tax incentives and low-interest loans to stimulate suburban home ownership, the construction of massive highway systems across the country linking city to suburb, along with low unemployment and a strong national economy, the growth of suburbs continued in earnest throughout the 1950's and into the 1960's (Fischer, 1984; Karp, Stone, & Yoels, 1991; Massey & Denton, 1993).

The Aftermath of City Depopulation

The 1970's brought about changes not only in the out-migration of residential populations from city to suburb but many businesses as well as companies began moving their operations to suburban locales (Karp, Stone, & Yoels, 1991). This movement coincided with a fundamental shift in the American economy from one in which the labor market was primarily involved in the manufacture and production of goods to one that was more service-oriented (Wilson, 1996). This shift spurred the closing of factories and the movement of jobs into the suburbs and eventually oversees as government policies, this time local in nature, provided tax and other business incentives to companies willing to relocate to suburban locales (Eitzen & Zinn, 1997; Karp, Stone, & Yoels, 1991). Moreover, companies whose business enterprise was rooted in the service industry did not need to be housed in large manufacturing plants, which tended to generate smoke or other pollutants and were generally situated near large bodies of water, but could instead conduct their business operations in office buildings which could be located in either the suburbs or the cities (Eitzen & Zinn, 1997).

The decline in the number of companies engaged in the manufacture and production of goods, along with the out-migration of manufacturing companies and many service-oriented businesses to the suburbs and eventually oversees resulted in a significant decline in the availability of manufacturing jobs within the cities, which had a devastating effect on the fortunes of low-skilled workers. As a consequence, many of these workers became trapped in a "spatial mismatch," in that, the manufacturing jobs in which they had acquired years of training and skill were becoming increasingly scarce and/or nonexistent within cities and they did not have the necessary training or skills to effectively compete for the high wage, high tech jobs that were becoming increasingly concentrated in the cities, nor did they have the necessary resources to move to those locales to which manufacturing jobs were still available (Gorham, 1992; Jargowsky, 1997; Wilson, 1980, 1987, 1996). Thus, faced with few options for gainful employment, many of these low-skilled workers sought employment within the service industry, the emerging predominate growth industry in the urban labor market (Jargowsky, 1997; Wilson, 1980, 1987, 1996). However, service-oriented jobs would prove to be both financially and occupationally unrewarding for many of these low-skilled workers as they typically paid at or near minimum wage, health benefits were poor or nonexistent, and these jobs were not a "stepping stone" for future higher-paying positions (Jargowsky, 1997; Wilson, 1980, 1987, 1996). In essence, most of these jobs proved to be "dead enders" providing no more today than they did the day before and offering few learning or training opportunities for advancement within the service industry or similar professions (Liebow, 1967; Wilson, 1996).

As a consequence of these city depopulation trends of both people and industry, cities gradually lost a significant number of their middle and upper income families and the revenues derived from the taxation of privately owned property and commercial establishments (Liska & Bellair, 1995; O'Donnell et al., 2002). Across the country, municipal services have borne the brunt of these revenue reductions as the quantity and quality of city services have been dramatically reduced in many regions of the country as local agencies and departments adapt to shrinking budgets (Liska & Bellair, 1995; O'Donnell et al., 2002; Wilson, 1987).

These declines in city services, coupled with a lack of fit between the skills of low-skilled city workers and the availability of commensurate employment options, have led to a number of interrelated urban problems including increased levels of joblessness, community disorder, residential instability, and concentrated poverty (Gorham, 1992; Gramlich, Laren, & Sealand, 1992; Jargowsky, 1997; Mouw, 2000; Wilson, 1987, 1996).

Social researchers that have studied the problems associated with deteriorating metropolitan communities have hypothesized that increased levels of social and community disorder undermines the viability of already fragile urban neighborhoods and provides visual cues of an erosion in neighborhood cohesion possibly signaling to community members and outsiders that previously unacceptable forms of behavior may now be tolerated and go unpunished (Sampson et al., 1999; Skogan, 1990; Wilson, 1987, 1996). In addition, prior social norms that regulated and controlled such behaviors may be replaced by emerging group norms that facilitate and encourage deviant activities (Anderson, 1991; Fagan, 1992). Hence, according to advocates of such beliefs, social and physical disorder, weak community bonds, and poor social networks increase the probability that negative social forces will take hold in such areas, potentially leading to an increase in untoward and illicit behavior (Sampson et al., 1999; Skogan, 1990; Wilson, 1987, 1996). Moreover, residents who live in such neighborhoods may feel socially and physically isolated and disconnected from the larger mainstream community (Fagan, 1992; Fernandez & Harris, 1992; Peterson & Harrell, 1992). Faced with limited prospects for gainful employment and surrounded by deviant and illicit behavior, they may become drawn to those activities that provide psychological, physical, and monetary rewards and that distract from their immediate circumstances, such as illicit substance use, drug trafficking, and other unlawful activities, placing them in jeopardy of progressing along a destructive pathway that, if left unchecked, may lead to drug dependence, family instability, violent behavior, multiple incarcerations, and premature death (Gorham, 1992; Hawkins et al., 1992, 1997; Kumpfer & Alvarado, 1998).

Baltimore City

Founded in 1797 on a branch of the Patapsco River, off the upper Chesapeake Bay, Baltimore, Maryland, the site of the present investigation, typifies the plight of America's older, large, post-industrial cities since the 1970s. Prior to and immediately following World War II, jobs within the manufacturing sector of the city's economy were plentiful as occupational opportunities grew in response to the demands of the wartime and later the postwar economy. During this time period, the population of Baltimore thrived and by 1950 the number of inhabitants living in the city slightly exceeded one million people. However, during the 1960s and 1970s, similar to declining population trends seen in other older, large, post-industrial east coast cities particularly Boston, Philadelphia, and Washington, D.C., Baltimore's population began to decline as suburban locales became more attractive to both individuals and businesses (Fischer, 1984; Karp, Stone, & Yoels, 1991; Massey & Denton, 1993; Taylor, 2000). This movement of both people and industry from city to suburb coincided with a fundamental shift in the American economy from one dominated primarily by industries involved in the manufacture and production of goods to one whose industries were predominately involved in high technology manufacturing, information processing, and service (Eitzen & Zinn, 1997; Gottdiener & Pickvance, 1991; Karp, Stone, & Yoels, 1991; Taylor, 2000; Wilson, 1996). This structural transformation (i.e., deindustrialization) of the American economy resulted in precipitous declines in manufacturing jobs in Baltimore and other older, large post-industrial cities throughout the United States from the 1970s through the 1990s (Gottdiener & Pickvance, 1991; Jargowsky, 1997; Massey & Denton, 1997; Taylor, 2000; Wilson, 1987). Such job losses, coupled with the outward migration of middle and working class families and industry from city to suburb (i.e., deconcentration) and a burgeoning illicit drug trade, contributed to a growth in concentrated poverty and other social ills in Baltimore and similar older, large, post-industrial cities in America (Gottdiener & Pickvance, 1991; Jargowsky, 1997; Karp, Stone, & Yoels, 1991; Mouw, 2000; Taylor, 2000; Wilson, 1996). Research has indicated that the deconcentration of both people and industry, urban joblessness, illicit drug trafficking and use, and concentrated poverty spawn a multiplicity of concomitant and interrelated social problems such as increased rates of delinquency, crime, and violence, and may ultimately result in reduced life chances for adults and youth living in such urban communities (Brooks-Gunn et al., 1997; Leventhal & Brooks-Gunn, 2000; Jargowsky, 1997; Mouw, 2000; Sampson & Laub, 1995; Wilson, 1987, 1996).

Summary

As a result of the complex and interrelated problems plaguing many of America's cities, African American youth living in such environments are exposed to a wide variety and an increasing number of serious social and environmental risk factors that may severely undermine their life chances and increase the likelihood that they will become involved in deviant activities (Aber et al., 1997; Bell & Jenkins, 1994, Dornbusch, et al., 2001; Kopstein & Roth, 1990; Kasarda, 1992; Grant et al., 2000; Huston et al., 1994; Wilson, 1996). The emergence and perpetuation of many of these social problems is directly attributable to, and symptomatic of, the decline in legitimate employment opportunities and the spread of concentrated poverty that has occurred in urban communities since the 1970s and 1980s (Jargowsky, 1997; Johnson et al., 1990; Mouw, 2000; Rankin & Quane, 2002, Wilson, 1987, 1996). Research has indicated that the deconcentration of both people and industry, urban joblessness, illicit drug trafficking and use, and concentrated poverty spawn a multiplicity of concomitant and interrelated social problems as a lack of available resources and increases in problem behaviors leads to higher rates of social disorganization characterized by delinquency, crime, and violence, ultimately resulting in reduced life chances for adults and youth living in such areas (Brooks-Gunn et al., 1997; Leventhal & Brooks-Gunn, 2000; Jargowsky, 1997; Mouw, 2000; Sampson & Laub, 1995; Wilson, 1987, 1996). The evidence regarding the considerable dangers that youth face in such environments and the high probability that they may participate in untoward and illicit activities appears quite compelling as

> Sociologists and criminologists have shown that the majority of juvenile crime occurs in densely populated urban neighborhoods, namely those nearest the city centers and those characterized by poverty, low economic opportunity, high residential mobility, physical deterioration, and disorganization (Ingoldsby & Shaw, 2002, p. 21).

Measurement Instruments & Items

I. Risk Behaviors

School performance problems

<u>YSRQ</u>

61. A. Have you ever gotten into trouble because of attendance, that is, not going to school when you are supposed to be there? Has that been...

Sometimes/Often = 1   Never = 0

61. B. Have you ever had to repeat a grade because you cut school or didn't go to class?

Yes = 1   No = 0

62. A. Have you ever had to repeat a grade because you failed?

Yes = 1   No = 0

67. A. What are your grades like in school? Mostly...

F's/D's = 1   C/B/A's = 0

CTRS-R

13. Not reading up to par

Little True/Pretty True/Very True = 1   Not True = 0

18. Lacks interest in schoolwork

Little True/Pretty True/Very True = 1   Not True = 0

22. Poor in arithmetic

Little True/Pretty True/Very True = 1   Not True = 0

CPRS-R

3. Difficulty doing or completing homework

Little True/Pretty True/Very True = 1   Not True = 0

8. Fails to complete assignments

Little True/Pretty True/Very True = 1   Not True = 0

CBCL

101. Truancy, skips school

Somewhat or Sometimes True/Very or Often True = 1

                                Not True = 0

TRF

61. Poor school work

Somewhat or Sometimes True/Very or Often True = 1

Not True = 0

(Total Number of Items: 11)

School conduct problems

YSRQ

63. A. How often have you been sent to the school guidance counselor or school psychologist? Has it been...

Sometimes/Often = 1   Never = 0

63. B. For what reason(s)

Attitude/Behavior = 1   Aca/Emo/Att/Otr = 0

64. A. Have you ever been suspended from school, that is, not allowed in the school for a certain amount of time and then allowed back in?

Yes = 1   No = 0

65. A. Have you ever been expelled from school, that is, forced to leave the school for good, not allowed back to that school?

Yes = 1   No = 0

CTRS-R

6. Actively defies or refuses to comply with adults' requests

Little True/Pretty True/Very True = 1   Not True = 0

15. Argues with adults

Little True/Pretty True/Very True = 1   Not True = 0

TRF

23. Disobedient at school.

Somewhat or Sometimes True/Very or Often True = 1

Not True = 0

37. Gets in many fights

Somewhat or Sometimes True/Very or Often True = 1

Not True = 0

(Total Number of Items: 8)

Use of ATODs

<u>YSRQ</u>

86. C1. Have you ever had a drink of beer, wine, or liquor, not just a sip of someone else's drink?

Yes = 1   No = 0

86. B1. Do you use tobacco products? (i.e., cigarettes, cigars, chewing tobacco, snuff)

Yes = 1   No = 0

87. Have you ever tried any of the following drugs not for medical reasons?

A. Inhalants, like glue

Yes = 1   No = 0

B. Marijuana or hashish

Yes = 1   No = 0

C. Other drugs? Specify

Yes = 1   No = 0

<u>TRF</u>

105. Uses alcohol or drugs for non-medical purposes (describe):

Somewhat or Sometimes True/Very or Often True = 1

Not True = 0

(Total Number of Items: 6)

Early involvement in risky sex

YSRQ

50. Have you ever had sexual activity with someone more than kissing or hugging?

Yes = 1   No = 0

(Total Number of Items: 1)

(Aggregate Total = 26)

II. Delinquency

Crimes of violence

YSRQ

81. W. Have you ever mugged anyone?

Yes = 1   No = 0

81. X. Have you ever shot at anyone with a gun?

Yes = 1   No = 0

81. BB. Have you ever robbed anyone using a weapon such as a gun or a knife?

Yes = 1   No = 0

(Total Number of Items: 3)

Crimes against property/person

<u>YSRQ</u>

81. A. Have you ever damaged or destroyed property that did not belong to you, for example, spray paint buildings, smash car windows, or slashed tires?

Yes = 1   No = 0

81. B. Have you ever "shook down" other kids for money, shoes, jacket(s), etc.?

Yes = 1   No = 0

81. F. Have you ever stole or tried to steal a bicycle?

Yes = 1   No = 0

81. G. Have you ever stole or tried to steal a motor vehicle such as a car or a motorcycle?

Yes = 1   No = 0

81. H. Have you ever shoplifted?

Yes = 1   No = 0

81. I. Have you ever stolen from school lockers, cash registers, mailboxes, vending machines, or places like that?

Yes = 1   No = 0

81. J. Have you ever snatched purses or picked pockets?

Yes = 1   No = 0

81. N. Have you ever broken into cars?

Yes = 1   No = 0

81. O. Have you ever broken into buildings, homes, or businesses?

Yes = 1   No = 0

81. V. Have you ever seriously hurt someone physically on purpose?

Yes = 1   No = 0

81. Z. Have you ever set things or property on fire?

Yes = 1   No = 0

CBCL

72. Sets fires

Somewhat or Sometimes True/Very or Often True = 1

Not True = 0

81. Steals at home

Somewhat or Sometimes True/Very or Often True = 1

Not True = 0

82. Steals outside the home

Somewhat or Sometimes True/Very or Often True = 1

Not True = 0

(Total Number of Items: 14)

Status offenses

YSRQ

34. G. Have you ever stayed out all night without permission?

Yes = 1   No = 0

60. Have your parents ever been asked to come to school because you missed school or misbehaved?

Yes = 1   No = 0

CBCL

67. Runs away from home

Somewhat or Sometimes True/Very or Often True = 1

                              Not True = 0

(Total Number of Items: 3)

Illicit drug possession/distribution

YSRQ

81. P. Have you ever sold drugs?

Yes = 1   No = 0

81. Q. Have you ever bought drugs for someone else?

Yes = 1   No = 0

81. R. Were you ever paid in money, gifts, or drugs, for delivering drugs?

Yes = 1   No = 0

81. S. Were you ever paid in money, gifts, or drugs, for keeping or holding drugs for someone else?

Yes = 1   No = 0

81. T. Were you ever paid in money, gifts or drugs, by a drug dealer to watch for the police?

Yes = 1   No = 0

(Total Number of Items: 5)

(Aggregate Total = 25)

III. Parental Attachment

Virtual supervision

<u>YSRQ</u>

26. D. Your mother trusts you

Disagree = 1   Agree = 0

30. D. Your father trusts you

Disagree = 1   Agree = 0

34. A. When you leave the house <u>during the day,</u> how often do you have to tell anyone where you're going and when you'll be back? Is that...
Never = 1   Al/Us/Half/Rare = 0

34. C. When you leave the house <u>at night,</u> how often do you have to tell anyone where you're going and when you will be back? Is that...

Never = 1   Al/Us/Half/Rare = 0

34. E. Do you have to be home by a certain time at night?

No = 1   Yes = 0

(Total Number of Items: 5)

Intimacy of communication

<u>YSRQ</u>

26. A. You enjoy talking things over with your mother

Disagree = 1   Agree = 0

26. B. You share your thoughts and feelings with your mother

Disagree = 1   Agree = 0

26. E. You can go to your mother for advice and guidance

Disagree = 1   Agree = 0

26. F. Your mother praises you or tells someone about it when you do something well

Disagree = 1   Agree = 0

30. A. You enjoy talking things over with your father

Disagree = 1   Agree = 0

30. B. You share your thoughts and feelings with your father

Disagree = 1   Agree = 0

30. E. You can go to your father for advice and guidance

Disagree = 1   Agree = 0

30. F. Your father praises you or tells someone about it when you do something well

Disagree = 1   Agree = 0

(Total Number of Items: 8)

Affectional identification

YSRQ

23. Would you like to be the kind of person your mother is when you're grown up

Disagree = 1   Agree = 0

26. C. Your mother understands your problems

Disagree = 1   Agree = 0

26. G. Your mother is too strict

Disagree = 0   Agree = 1

26. H. Your mother is always picking on you

Disagree = 0   Agree = 1

27. Would you like to be the kind of person your father is when you're grown up

Disagree = 1   Agree = 0

30. C. Your father understands your problems

Disagree = 1   Agree = 0

30. G. Your father is too strict

Disagree = 0   Agree = 1

30. H. Your father is always picking on you

Disagree = 0   Agree = 1

(Total Number of Items: 8)

Joint/leisure involvement

<u>YSRQ</u>

40. About how often does your family sit down and eat dinner together? About how many days per week or month is that?

Never = 1   Week/Month = 0

41. About how often does/do your parent(s) take you out just for fun or recreation, like to a park, a movie, to eat out, to a sports event, or some other amusement? About how many days per week or month is that?

Never = 1   Week/Month = 0

(Total Number of Items: 2)

(Aggregate Total = 23)

IV. Family Socioeconomic Status

<u>CQ</u>

Parental education

4. What was the last year of education that you completed?

> Professional Degree = 1
> Four-year College Graduate = 2

One to three years college and business school = 3
High School Graduate/GED or less = 4

(Total Number of Items: 4)

Parental occupation

12. A. Over the past year, what have you done for a living:
what has been your main job?

Higher Execs and Major Professionals = 1
Business Mgrs, Admin, and Lesser Pros = 2
Small Bus Owners, Clerical, Techs, Sales = 3
Skilled Manual Employees = 4
Semi-Skilled = 5
Unskilled employees = 6
Homemaker = 7
Student, disabled, no occupation = 8

(Total Number of Items: 8)

Family income

18. What would you estimate your annual household
income to be?

Above $50,000 = 1
Above $40,000 but below $50,000 = 2
Above $30,000 but below $40,000 = 3
Above $20,000 but below $30,000 = 4
Above $10,000 but below $20,000 = 5
Below $10,000 = 6

(Total Number of Items: 6)

V. Deviant Peer Relationships

Associations with deviant peers

<u>YSRQ</u>

66. Have any of your close friends ever been expelled from school

Yes = 1   No = 0

84. A. How many of your close friends have ever damaged or destroyed property that did not belong to them, for example, spray paint buildings, smash car windows, slash tires?

Yes = 1   No = 0

84. B. How many of your close friends have ever "shook down" other kids for money, shoes, jacket(s), etc.?

Yes = 1   No = 0

84. F. How many of your close friends have ever stolen or tried to steal a bicycle?

Yes = 1   No = 0

84. G. How many of your close friends have ever stolen or tried to steal a motor vehicle such as a car or a motorcycle?

Yes = 1   No = 0

84. H. How many of your close friends have ever shoplifted?

Yes = 1   No = 0

84. I. How many of your close friends have ever stolen from school lockers, cash registers, mailboxes vending machines, or places like that?

Yes = 1   No = 0

84. J. How many of your close friends have ever snatched purses or picked pockets?

Yes = 1   No = 0

84. N. How many of your close friends have ever broken into cars?

Yes = 1   No = 0

84. O. How many of your close friends have ever broken into buildings, homes, or businesses?

Yes = 1   No = 0

84. P. How many of your close friends have ever sold drugs?

Yes = 1   No = 0

84. R. How many of your close friends were ever paid in money, gifts or drugs, for delivering drugs?

Yes = 1   No = 0

84. S. How many of your close friends were ever paid in money, gifts or drugs, for keeping or holding drugs for someone else?

Yes = 1   No = 0

84. T. How many of your close friends were ever paid in money, gifts or drugs, by a drug dealer to watch for the police?

Yes = 1   No = 0

84. V. How many of your close friends have ever seriously hurt someone physically on purpose?

Yes = 1   No = 0

84. W. How many of your close friends have ever mugged anyone?

Yes = 1   No = 0

84. X. How many of your close friends have ever shot at anyone with a gun?

Yes = 1   No = 0

84. Z. How many of your close friends have ever set things or property on fire?

Yes = 1   No = 0

84. BB. How many of your close friends have ever robbed anyone using a weapon such as a gun or a knife?

Yes = 1   No = 0

TRF

39. Hangs around with others who get in trouble

Somewhat or Sometimes True/Very or Often True = 1

Not True = 0

(Total Number of Items: 20)

References

Aber, J. L., Bennett, N. G., Li, J., & Conley, D. C. (1997). The effects of poverty on child health and development. *Annual Review of Public Health, 18*, 463-483.

Achenbach, T. M. (1982). *Developmental psychopathology.* New York: Wiley.

Achenbach, T. M., & Edelbrock, C. S. (1987). *Manual for the child behavior checklist and revised child behavior profile.* Burlington, VT: University of Vermont.

Achenbach, T. M. (1991). *Manual for the teacher's report form and 1991 profile.* Burlington, VT: University of Vermont.

Adams, M. S., Robertson, C. T., Gray-Ray, P., & Ray, M. C. (2003). Labeling and delinquency. *Adolescence, 38,* 171-86.

Agnew, R. (1985). Social control theory and delinquency: A longitudinal test. *Criminology, 23,* 47-61.

Agnew, R. (1991). The interactive effect of peer variables on delinquency. *Criminology, 29,* 47-72.

Agnew, R. (1991). A longitudinal test of social control theory and delinquency. *Journal of Research in Crime and Delinquency, 28,* 126-156.

Agnew, R. (2001). Building on the foundation of general strain theory: Specifying the types of strain most likely to lead to delinquency. *Journal of Research in Crime and Delinquency, 38,* 319-361.

Akers, R. L. (1997). *Criminological theories: Introduction and evaluation* (2nd ed.). Los Angeles: Roxbury Publishing Co.

Albert, N., & Beck, A. T. (1975). Incidence of depression in early adolescence: A preliminary study. *Journal of Youth and Adolescence, 4,* 301-307.

Anderson, J. G. (1987). Structural equation models in the social and behavioral sciences: Model building. *Child Development, 58,* 49-64.

Anderson, E. (1991). Neighborhood effects on teenage pregnancy. In C. Jencks & P. E. Peterson (Eds.), *The urban underclass* (pp. 375-398). Washington, DC: The Urban Institute.

Anglin, M. D., & Speckart, G. (1986). Narcotics use, property crime and dealing: Structural dynamics across the addiction career. *Journal of Quantitative Criminology, 2,* 335-375.

Anglin, M. D., & Speckart, G. (1988). Narcotics use and crime: A multisample, multimethod analysis. *Criminology, 26,* 197-233.

Arbona, C., & Power, T. G. (2003). Parental Attachment, self-esteem, and antisocial behaviorsamong African American, European American, and Mexican American adolescents. *Journal of Counseling Psychology, 50(1),* 40-51.

Asher, H. B., (1983). *Causal modeling* (2nd ed.). Newbury Park, CA: Sage Publications.

Babbie, E. (1995). *The practice of social research* (7th ed.). Belmont, CA: Wadsworth Publishing.

Babbie, E. (2004). *The practice of social research* (10th ed.). Belmont, CA: Wadsworth Publishing.

Barber, B. K., & Rollins, B. C. (1990). *Parent-adolescent relationships.* Lanham, MD: University Press of America.

Barber, B. K., Olsen, J. E. & Shagle, S. C. (1994). Association between parental psychological and behavioral control and youth internalized and externalized behaviors. *Child Development, 65,* 1120-1136.

Barnes, G. M., & Welte, J. W. (1986). Patterns and predictors of alcohol use among 7-12th-grade students in New York State. *Journal of Studies on Alcohol, 47,* 53-62.

Barnow, S., Lucht, M., & Freyberger, H. J. (2005). Correlates of aggressive and delinquent conduct problems in adolescence. *Wiley Interscience* (www.interscience.wiley.com), *31,* 24-39.

Barone, C., Ickovics, J., Ayers, T., Katz, S., Voyce, C., & Weissberg, R. (1996). High-risk sexual behavior among young urban students. *Family Planning Perspectives, 28,* 69-74.

Bauman, K. E., Foshee, V. A., Linzer, M. A., & Koch, G. G. (1990). The effect of parental smoking classification on the association between parental and adolescent smoking. *Addictive Behaviors, 15,* 413-422.

Bell, C. C., & Jenkins, E. J. (1993). Community violence and children on Chicago's Southside. *Psychiatry, 56,* 46-54.

Beier, S., Rosenfeld, W., Spitalny, K., Zansky, S., & Bontemp, A. (2000). The potential role of an adult mentor in influencing high-risk behavior in adolescents. *Annals of Pediatrics and Adolescent Medicine, 154,* 327-331.

Bell-Scott, P. (1990). Family-adolescent relationships. In V. McBride Murry (Ed.), *Black adolescence: Current issues and annotated bibliography* (pp. 109-124). Boston: G. K. Hall & Co.

Bell, C. C., & Jenkins, E. J. (1994). Community violence and children on Chicago's southside. *Psychiatry, 56*, 46-54.

Bellair, P. E., & Roscigno, V. J. (2000). Local labor-market opportunity and adolescent delinquency. *Social Forces, 78*, 1509-1539.

Bennett, C., & Harris, J. J. (1982). Suspension and expulsions of male and Black students: A study of the causes of disproportionality. *Urban Education, 16*, 399-423.

Bentler, P. M. (1990). Comparative fit indexes in structural models. *Psychometrika, 107*, 238-246.

Bentler, P. M., and C. P. Chou (1987). Practical issues in structural modeling. *Sociological Methods and Research, 16*, 78-117.

Bérubé, R. L., & Achenbach, T. M. (2001). *Bibliography of published studies using ASEBA instruments: 2001 edition*. Burlington, VT: University of Vermont.

Billingsley, A. (1992). *Climbing Jacob's ladder: The enduring legacy of African American families*. New York: Simon & Schuster.

Black, M., & Ricardo, I. (1994). Drug use, drug trafficking, and weapon carrying among low-income, African-American, early adolescent boys. *Pediatrics, 94*, 1065-1072.

Blau, J., & Blau, P (1982). The cost of inequality: Metropolitan structure and violent crime. *American Sociological Review, 47*, 114-128.

Blake, S. M., Amaro, H., Schwartz, P. M., & Flinchbaugh, L. J. (2001). A review of substance abuse prevention interventions for young adolescent girls. *Journal of Early Adolescence, 21*, 294-324.

Blitsten, J. L., Murray, D. M., Lytle, L. A., Birnbaum, A. S., & Perry, C. L. (2005). Predictors of violent behavior in an early adolescent cohort: Similarities and differences across genders. *Health Education and Behavior, 32(2)*, 175-194.

Bollen, K. A. (1989). A new incremental fit index for general structural equation models. *Sociological Methods & Research, 17*, 303-316.

Borden, L. M., Donnermeyer, J. F., & Scheer, S. D. (2001). The influence of extra-curricular activities and peer influence on substance use. *Adolescent and Family Health, 2(1)*, 12-19.

Borduin, C. M., Pruitt, J. A., & Henggeler, S. W. (2001). Family interactions in Black, lower-class families with delinquent and nondelinquent adolescent boys. *Journal of Genetic Psychology, 147*, 333-342.

Box, S. (1987). *Recession, crime and punishment*. London, England: Macmillan.

Boyer, C. B., Shafer, M. A., Wibbelsman, C. J., Seeberg, D., Teitle, E., & Lovell, N. (2000). Associations of sociodemographic, psychosocial, and behavioral factors with sexual risk and sexually transmitted diseases in teen clinic patients. *Journal of Adolescent Health, 27*, 102-111.

Bradley, R. H., & Corwyn, R. F. (2002). Socioeconomic status and child development. *Annual Review of Psychology, 53*, 371-399.

Brooks-Gunn, J., Duncan, G., & Aber, J. L. (1997). *Neighborhood poverty. Volume I: Context and consequences for children*. New York: Russell Sage Foundation.

Brough, P., & Frame, R. (2004). Predicting police job satisfaction and turnover intentions: The role of social support and police organizational variables. *New Zealand Journal of Psychology, 33*, 8-16.

Brounstein, P., Zweig, J., & Gardner, S. (2001a). Science- based substance abuse prevention programs: A guide. In *guide to science-based practices, Vol. 1* (Publication No. SMA 01-3506). Washington, DC: Department of Health and Human Services.

Brounstein, P., Zweig, J., & Gardner, S. (2001b). Promising and proven substance abuse prevention programs. In *Guide to Science-Based Practices, Vol. 2* (Publication No. SMA 01-3506). Washington, DC: Department of Health and Human Services.

Brown, B. (2004). Adolescents' relationships with peers. In R. Lerner & L. Steinberg (Eds.),*Handbook of adolescent psychology* (pp. 363–394). New York: Wiley.

Brown, B. G., Eicher, S. A., & Petrie, S. (1986). The importance of peer ("crowd") affiliation in adolescence. *Journal of Adolescence, 9*, 73-96.

Browne, M. W., & Cudeck, R. (1993). Alternative ways of assessing model fit. In K. A. Bollen & J.S. Long (Eds.), Testing structural equation models (pp. 136-162). Newbury Park, CA: Sage.

Bollen, & J. S. Long (Eds.), *Testing structural equation models* (pp. 136-162). Thousand Oaks, CA: Sage.

Buist, K. L., Dekovic, M., Meeus, W., & van Aken, M. A. G. (2004). The reciprocal relationship between early adolescent attachment and internalizing and externalizing problem behaviour. *Journal of Adolescence, 27*, 251-266.

Bry, B., & Krinsley, K. (1990). *Adolescent substance abuse. Adolescent behavior therapy handbook.* New York: Springer Publishing Company, Inc.

Canter, R. J. (1982). Sex differences in self-report delinquency. *Criminology, 20,* 373-393.

Canter, R. J. (1982). Family correlates of male and female delinquency. *Criminology, 20,* 167.

Capaldi, D., & Patterson, G. (1994). Interrelated influences of contextual factors in antisocial behavior in adulthood and adolescence for males. In D. Fowels & P. Sutker (Eds.), *Experimental personality and psychotherapy research* (pp. 165-198). New York: Springer Publications.

Centers, N. L., & Weist, M. D. (1998). Inner city youth and drug dealing: A review of the problem. *Journal of Youth and Adolescence, 27(3),* 395-411.

Centers for Disease Control and Prevention (2000). Youth risk behavior surveillance—United States, 1999. *Morbidity and Mortality Weekly Report, 49 (SS05),* 1-96.

Cernkovich, S. A., & Giordano, P. C. (1987). Family relationships and delinquency. *Criminology, 25,* 295-321.

Chaiken, J. M., & Chaiken, M. R. (1982). *Varieties of criminal behavior: Summary and policy implications.* Santa Monica: Rand.

Chaiken, J. M., & Chaiken, M. R. (1990). Drugs and predatory crime. In M. Tonry & J. Q. Wilson (Eds.), *Drugs and crime* (pp. 203-39). Chicago: University of Chicago Press.

Chapple, C. L., McQuillan, J. A., & Berdahl, T. A. (2004). Gender, social bonds, and delinquency: A comparison of boys' and girls' models. *Social Science Research, 34,* 357-383.

Chase-Lansdale, P. L., & Pittman, L. D. (2002). Welfare reform and parenting: Reasonable expectations. In M.K. Shields (Ed.), *Future of Children: Children and Welfare Reform* (pp. 167-183). Los Altos, CA: The David and Lucile Packard Foundation.

Chesney-Lind, M. (1986). Women and crime: The female offender. *Signs, 12,* 78-96.

Chesney-Lind, M., & Shelden, R. G. (1992). *Girls, delinquency, and juvenile justice.* Pacific Grove, CA: Brooks/Cole.

Chesney-Lind, M. (1997). *The female offender.* Thousand Oaks, CA: Sage.

Chesney-Ling, M. (2002). Criminalizing victimization: The unintended consequences of pro-arrest politics for girls and women. *Criminology and Public Policy, 2*, 81-90.

Children's Defense Fund (1995). *The state of America's children.* Washington, DC: Author.

Children's Defense Fund (2002). *The state of America's children.* Washington, DC: Author.

Chung, H. L., & Steinberg, L. (2006). Relations between neighborhood factors, parenting behaviors, peer deviance, and delinquency among serious juvenile offenders. *Developmental Psychology, 42(2)*, 319-331.

Clubb, P. A., Browne, D. C., Humphrey, A. D., Schoenbach, V., Meyer, B., & Jackson, M. (2001). Violent behaviors in early adolescent minority youth: Results from a middle school youth risk behavior survey. *Maternal and Child Health Journal, 5(4)*, 225-235.

Cohen, J. W. (1988). *Statistical power analysis for the behavioral sciences* (2nd ed.). Hillsdale, NJ: Lawrence Erlbaum Associates.

Cohen, D., Spear, Scribner, R., Kissinger, P., Mason, & Wildgen, J. (2000). Broken windows and the risk of gonorrhea. *American Journal of Public Health, 90*, 230-236.

Collins, P. H. (1991). *Black feminist thought: Knowledge, consciousness, and the politics of empowerment.* New York: Routledge.

Conger, R. D. (1976). Social control and social learning models of delinquent behavior: A synthesis. *Criminology, 14*, 17-40.

Conners, C. K., (1997). *Conners' rating scales – revised technical manual.* North Tonawanda, NY: Multi-Health Systems Inc.

Cooley-Quille, M., Boyd, R. C., Frantz, E., & Walsh, J. (2001). Emotional and behavioral impact of exposure to community violence in inner-city adolescents. *Journal of Clinical Child Psychology, 30(1)*, 199-206.

Coughlin, C., & Vuchinich, S. (1996). Family experience in preadolescence and the development of male delinquency. *Journal of Marriage & Family, 58*, 491-502.

Crane, J. (1991). Effects of neighborhoods on dropping out of school and teenage childbearing. In C. Jencks & P. E. Peterson (Eds.), *The urban underclass* (pp. 299-320). Washington, DC: The Urban Institute.

Crowley, T. J., & Riggs, P. D. (1995). Adolescent substance use disorder with conduct disorder and comorbid conditions. In Rahdert, E., Czechowicz, D., eds. *Adolescent Drug Abuse: Clinical Assessment and Therapeutic Interventions.* NIDA Research Monograph 156. Rockville, MD: National Institute on Drug Abuse, pp. 49-111.

Crutchfield, R. D. (1989). Labor stratification and violent crime. *Social Forces, 68,* 489-512.

Daly, K. (1994). *Gender crime and punishment.* New Haven, CT: Yale University Press.

Daane, D. M. (2003). Child and adolescent violence. Orthopaedic Nursing, 22(1), 23-31.

Davis, N. (1999). *Resilience: Status of the research and research-based programs.* Rockville, MD: Substance Abuse and Mental Health Services Administration.

Dembo, R., Grandon, G., LaVoie, L., Schmeidler, J., & Burgos, W. (1986). Parents and drugs revisited: Some further evidence in support of social learning theory. *Criminology, 24,* 85-104.

Dembo, R., Williams, L., Schmeidler, J., Wish, E., Getreu, A., & Berry, E. (1991). Juvenile crime and drug abuse: A prospective study of high risk youth. *Journal of Addiction Disorders, 11,* 5-31.

Dickerson, B. J. (1995). *African American single mothers: Understanding their lives and families.* Thousand Oaks, CA: Sage.

DiClemente, R. J., Wingood, G. M., Crosby, R. A., Sionean, C., Cobb, B. K., Harrington, K., Davies, S. L., Hook, E. W., & Oh, M. K. (2002). Sexual risk behaviors associated with having older sex partners: A study of black adolescent females. *Sexually Transmitted Diseases, 29,* 20-24.

Dishion, T. J. (1990). The family ecology of boys peer relations in middle childhood. *Child Development, 61,* 874-892.

Dishion, T. J., Andrews, D. W., & Crosby, L. (1995a). Antisocial boys and their friends in early adolescence: Relationship characteristics, quality, and interactional processes. *Child Development, 66,* 139-151.

Dishion, T. J., Capaldi, D., Spracklen, K. M., & Li, F. (1995b). Peer ecology of male adolescent drug use. *Development & Psychopathology, 7,* 803-824.

Dodge, K. A., Petit, G. S., & Bates, J. E. (1994). Socialization mediators of the relation between socioeconomic status and child conduct problems. *Child Development, 65,* 649-665.

Doljanac, R. F., & Zimmerman, M. A. (1998). Psychosocial factors and high-risk sexual behavior: Race differences among urban adolescents. *Journal of Behavioral Medicine, 21*, 451-467.

Donohew, R. L., Hoyle, R. H., Clayton, R. R., Skinner, W. F., Colon, S. E., & Rice, R. E. (1999). Sensation seeking and drug use by adolescents and their friends: Models for marijuana and alcohol. *Journal of Studies on Alcohol, 60*, 622-631.

Donovan, J. E., & Jessor, R. (1985). Structure of problem behavior in adolescence and young adulthood. *Journal of Consulting and Clinical Psychology, 53*, 890-904.

Dornbusch, S. M., Erickson, K. G., Laird, J., & Wong, C. A. (2001). The relation of family and school attachment to adolescent deviance in diverse groups and communities. *Journal of Adolescent Research, 16*, 396-422.

Dryfoos, J. (1991). Preventing high-risk behavior. *American Journal of Public Health, 81*, 175-158.

Dunaway, G., Cullen, F. T., Burton, V. S., & Evans, T. D. (2000). The myth of social class and crime revisited: An examination of class and adult criminality. *Criminology, 38*, 589-632.

Duncan, G. J., & Hoffman, S. D. (1991). Teenage underclass behavior and subsequent poverty: Have the rules changed? In C. Jencks & P.E. Peterson (Eds.), *The urban underclass* (pp. 155-174). Washington, DC: The Urban Institute.

Duncan, G., & Yeung, W. (1995). Extent and consequences of welfare dependence among America's children. *Children & Youth Services Review, 17*, 157-182.

Dunn, G., Everitt, B., & Pickles, A. (1993). *Modelling covariances and latent variables using EQS*. Boca Raton, FL: Chapman & Hall/CRC.

Dunst, C. J., & Trivette, C. (1994). Methodological considerations and strategies for studying the long-term follow-up of early intervention. In S. Friedman & H. Haywood (Eds.), *Developmental follow-up: Concepts, domains, and methods* (pp. 277-313). San Diego, CA: Academic Press.

Durant, R. H., Cadenhead, C., Pendergrast, R. A., Slavens, G., & Linder, C. W. (1994). Factors associated with the use of violence among black adolescents. *American Journal of Public Health, 84*, 612-617.

Edelman, M. W. (1995). United we stand: A common vision. *Claiming Children, 1*, 6-12.

Eitzen, D. S., & Zinn, M. B. (1997). *Social problems* (7[th]ed.). Boston: Allyn and Bacon.

Elliott, D. S., Huizinga, D., & Ageton, S. S. (1985). *Explaining delinquency and drug use.* Newbury Park, CA: Sage Publications, Inc.

Elliott, D. S., Huizinga, D., & Menard, S. (1989). *Multiple problem youth: Delinquency, substance use, and mental health problems.* New York: Springer-Verlag.

Elliott, D. (1994). Serious violent offenders: Onset, development course, and termination. *Criminology, 32,* 1-21.

Empey, L. T. (1982). *American delinquency.* Homewood, IL: Dorsey.

Epstein, J. A., Botvin, G. J., Baker, E., & Diaz, T. (1999). Impact of social influences and problem behavior on alcohol use among inner-city Hispanic and Black adolescents. *Journal of Studies on Alcohol, 60,* 595-604.

Epstein, J. A., Botvin, G. J., Griffin, K. W., & Diaz, T. (1999). Role of ethnicity and gender in polydrug use among a longitudinal sample of inner-city adolescents. *Journal of Alcohol and Drug Education, 45,* 1-12.

Fagan, J. (1993). Interactions among drugs, alcohol, and violence. *Health Affirmations, 12,* 65-79.

Farrell, A. D., & Bruce, S. E. (1997). Impact of exposure to community violence on violent behavior and emotional distress among urban adolescents. *Journal of Clinical Child Psychology, 26(1),* 2-14.

Farrington, D. (1987). Implications of biological findings for criminological research. In S. Mednick, T. Moffitt, & S. Stack (Eds.), *Causes of crime.* Cambridge, MA: Cambridge University Press.

Farrington, D. P., Loeber, R., Yin, Y., & Anderson, S. (2002). Are within-individual causes of delinquency the same as between-individual causes? *Criminal Behaviour and Mental Health, 12,* 53-68.

Feagin, J. R., & Vera, H. (1995). *White racism: The basics.* New York: Routledge.

Fergusson, D., Lynskey, M., & Horwood, L. (1996). Alcohol misuse and juvenile offending in adolescents. *Addiction, 91,* 483-494.

Fergusson, D., Swain-Campbell, N., & Horwood, J. (2004). How does childhood economic disadvantage lead to crime? *Journal of Child Psychology and Psychiatry, 45(5),* 956-966.

Fernandez, R., & Harris, D. (1992). Social isolation and the underclass. In A. V. Harrell & G.E. Peterson (Eds.), *Drugs, crime and social isolation: Barriers to urban opportunity* (pp. 257-294). Washington, DC: Urban Institute Press.

Fischer, C. S. (1984). *The urban experience* (2nd ed.). Fort Worth, TX: Harcourt Brace Jovanovich, Inc.

Fortenberry, J. (1998). Alcohol, drugs, and STD/HIV risk among adolescents. *AIDS Patient care and STD's, 12*, 783-786.

Foshee, V., & Baumna, K. E. (1992). Parental and peer characteristics as modifiers of the bond-behavior relationship: An elaboration of control theory. *Journal of Health and Social Behavior, 33*, 66-76.

Fowles, D. C., & Kochanska, G. (2000). Temperament as a moderator of pathways to conscience in children: The contribution of electrodermal activity. *Psychophysiology, 37*, 788-795.

Fraser, M., Richman, J., & Galinsky, M. (1999). Risk, protection, and resilience: Towards a conceptual framework for social work practice. *Social Work Research, 23*, 131-144.

Freedman, M. (1993). Freedman's 1993 review of U.S. mentoring programs: Selected findings and observations. *Intervention in School & Clinic, 32*, 205.

Freudenberg, N., Richie, R. L., Taylor, R. T., McGillicuddy, K., & Greene, M. B. (1999). Coming up in the boogie down: The role of violence in the lives of adolescents in the South Bronx. *Health Education Behaviors, 26*, 788-805.

Friedman, J., & Rosenbaum, D. P. (1988). Social control theory: The salience of components by age, gender, and type of crime. *Journal of Quantitative Criminology, 4*, 363-380.

Gallay, L. S., & Flanagan, C. A. (2000). The well-being of children in a changing economy: Time for a new social contract in America. In R. D. Taylor & M. C. Wang (Eds.), *Resilience across contexts: Work, family, culture, and community* (pp. 3-33). Mahwah, NJ: Lawrence Erlbaum.

Garbarino, J., Dubrow, N., Kostelny, K., & Pardo, C. (1991). *Children in Danger: Coping with the consequences of community violence.* San Francisco, CA: Jossey-Bass.

Garbarino, J. (1995a). The American war zone: What children can tell us about living with violence. *Journal of Deviant Behavior Pediatrics, 16*, 431-435.

Garbarino, J. (1995b). Growing up in a socially toxic environment: Life for children and families in the 1990s. *Nebr Symp Motiv, 42,* 1-20.

Garmezy, N. (1985). Stress-resistant children: The search for protective factors. In J. Stevenson (Ed.), *Recent research in development psychopathology* (pp. 213-233). New York: Elsevier Science.

Garmezy, N. (1991). Resilience and vulnerability to adverse developmental outcomes associated with poverty. *American Behavioral Scientist, 34,* 416-430.

Gavazzi, S. M., Yarcheck, C. M., & Lim, J. Y. (2005). Ethnicity, gender, and global risk indicators in the lives of status offenders coming to the attention of the juvenile court. International Journal of Offender *Therapy and Comparative Criminology, 49(6),* 696-710.

George, S. M., & Dickerson, B. J. (1995). The role of the grandmother in poor single-mother families and households. In B. J. Dickerson (Ed.), *African American single mothers: Understanding their lives and families* (pp. 146-163). Thousand Oaks, CA: Sage.

Gibbs, J. T., Brunswick, A. F., Connor, M. E., Dembo, R., Larson, T. E., Reed, R. J., & Solomon, B. (1988). *Young, Black, and male in America: An endangered species.* Dover, MA: Auburn House.

Giordano, P. G., & Cernkovich, S. A. (1993). The family and peer relations of Black adolescents. *Journal of Marriage & Family, 55,* 277-288.

Glueck, S., & Glueck, E. (1950). *Unraveling juvenile delinquency.* Cambridge, MA: Harvard University Press.

Glueck, S., & Glueck, E. (1968). *Delinquents and Nondelinquents in Perspective.* Cambridge: Harvard University Press.

Goldstein, P. J., Hunt, D., Des Jarlais, D. C., & Deren, S. (1987). Drug dependence and abuse. In R. W. Amler & H. B. Dull (Eds.), *Closing the gap: The burden of unnecessary illness (pp. 9-18).* New York: Oxford University Press.

Gorham, W. (1992). Forward. In A. V. Harrell & G. E. Peterson (Eds.), *Drugs, Crime, and Social Isolation: Barriers to Urban Opportunity* (xviii). Washington, DC: Urban Institute Press.

Gottfredson, D. C. (1987). An evaluation of an organization development approach to reducing school disorder. *Evaluation Review, 11,* 739-763.

Gottfredson, D. C. (2001). *Schools and delinquency.* New York: Cambridge University Press.

Gottdiener, M., & Pickvance, C. G. (1991). *Urban Life in Transition (Urban Affairs Annual Reviews).* Beverly Hills, CA: Sage.

Gramlich, E., Laren, D., & Sealand, N. (1992). Mobility into and out of poor urban neighborhoods. In A. V. Harrell & G. E. Peterson (Eds.), *Drugs, crime and social isolation: Barriers to urban opportunity* (pp. 241-256). Washington, DC: Urban Institute Press.

Grant, K. E., O'Koon, J. H., Davis, T. H., Roache, N.A., Poindexter, L. M., Armstrong, M. L., Minden, J. A., & McIntosh, J. M. (2000). Protective factors affecting low-income urban African American youth exposed to stress. *Journal of Adolescence, 20,* 388-418.

Green, S., & Babyak, M. (1997). Control of type I errors with multiple tests of constraints in structural equation modeling. *Multivariate Behavioral Research, 32,* 39-51.

Greenberg, D. F. (1999). The weak strength of social control theory. *Crime & Delinquency, 45,* 66-182.

Grunbaum, J., Kann, L., Kinchen, S., Williams, B., Ross, J., & Lowry, R. (2002). Youth risk behavior surveillance: United States, 2001. *Morbidity & Mortality Weekly Report, 51*(SS-4), 1-62.

Guo, J., Hill, K. G., Hawkins, J. D., Catalano, R. F., & Abbott, R. D. (2002). A developmental analysis of sociodemographic, family, and peer effects on adolescent illicit drug initiation. *Journal of the American Academy of Child and Adolescent Psychiatry, 41,* 838-845.

Hagan, J. (1992). The poverty of a classless criminology—The American society of criminology 1991 presidential address. *Criminology, 30,* 1-19.

Hagan, J., & Foster, H. (2003). S/He's a rebel: Toward a sequential stress theory of delinquency and gendered pathways to disadvantage in emerging adulthood. *Social Forces, 82,* 53-86.

Hartjen, C. A., & Priyadarsini, S. (2003). Gender, peers, and delinquency: A study of boys and girls in rural France. *Youth & Society, 34,* 387-414.

Hastings, P.D., Zahn-Waxler, C., Robinson, J., Usher, D., & Bridges, D. (2000). The development of concern for others in children with behavior problems. *Developmental Psychology, 36,* 531-546.

Hawkins, J. D., Catalano, R. F., & Miller, J. (1992). Risk and protective factors for alcohol and other drug problems in adolescence and early adulthood: Implications for substance abuse prevention. *Psychological Bulletin, 112,* 64-105.

Hawkins, J. D., Arthur, M. W., & Olson, J. J. (1997). Community interventions to reduce risks and enhance protection against antisocial behavior. In D. W. Stoff, J.Brieling, & J. D. Masers (Eds.), *Handbook of antisocial behavior* (pp. 365-374). New York: John Wiley & Sons.

Hawkins, J. D., Graham, J. W., Maguin, E., Abbott, R. D., Hill, K. G., & Catalano, R. F.(1997). Exploring the effects of age of alcohol use initiation and psychosocial risk factors on subsequent alcohol misuse. *Journal of Studies on Alcohol, 58,* 280-290.

Hawkins, J. D., Kosterman, R., Maguin, E., Catalano, R., & Arthur, M. W. (1997).Preventive interventions: Substance use, misuse, and abuse. In R. T. Ammerman & M. Hersen (Eds.), *Handbook of prevention and treatment with children and adolescents: Intervention in the real world context* (pp. 203-237). New York: John Wiley & Sons.

Hawkins, J., Catalano, R., Kosterman, R., Abbott, R., & Hill, K. (1999). Preventing adolescent health-risk behaviors by strengthening protection during childhood. *Archives of Pediatric and Adolescent Medicine, 153,* 226-234.

Haynie, D. L. (2001). Delinquent peers revisited: Does network structure matter? *American Journal of Sociology, 106,* 1013-1058.

Haynie, D. L., & Osgood, D. W. (2005). Reconsidering peers and delinquency: How do peers matter? *Social Forces, 84(2),* 1109-1130.

Haynie, D. L., Silver, E., & Teasdale, B. (2006). Neighborhood characteristics, peer networks, and adolescent violence. *Journal of Quantitative Criminology, 22,* 147-169.

Healey, J. (2001). *Statistics: A tool for social research.* Belmont, CA: Wadsworth.

Heimer, K. (1997). Socioeconomic status, subcultural definitions, and violent delinquency. *Social Forces, 75,* 799-834.

Heinze, H. J., Toro, P. A., & Urberg, K. A. (2004). Antisocial behavior and affiliation with deviant peers. *Journal of Clinical Child and Adolescent Psychology, 33 (2),* 336-346.

Henggeler, S. W. (1989). *Delinquency in adolescents: Developmental Clinical Psychology and Psychiatry Series, 18*. Newbury Park, CA: Sage Publications.

Henry, D. B. (2001). Longitudinal family and peer group effects on violence and nonviolent delinquency. *Journal of Clinical Child Psychology, 30*, 172-187.

Hepburn, J. R. (1976). Criminology: Testing alternative models of delinquent causation. *Journal of Criminal Law and Criminology, 67*, 450-460.

Herjanic, B. M., Barredo, V. H., Herjanic, M., & Tomelleri, C. J. (1979). Children of heroin addicts. *International Journal of the Addictions, 14,* 919-931.

Herrenkohl, T. I., Maguin, E., Hill, K. G., Hawkins, J. D., Abbott, R. D., & Catalano, R. F. (2000). Developmental risk factors for youth violence. *Society for Adolescent Medicine, 26*, 176-186.

Herskovits, M. J. (1958). *The myth of the Negro past*. Boston: Beacon Press.

Hill, R. B. (1997). *The strengths of African American families: Twenty-five years later*. Washington, DC: R & B Publishers.

Hindelang, M. J. (1973). Causes of delinquency: A partial explication and extension. *Social Problems, 20*, 471-487.

Hirschi, T. (1969). *Causes of delinquency*. New Brunswick, NJ: Transaction Publishers.

Hoffmann, J. P. (2003). A contextual analysis of differential association, social control, and strain theories of delinquency. *Social Forces, 81*, 753-786.

Hollingshead, A. B. (1975). *Four factor index of social status*. New Haven, CT: Yale University.

Howard, D., Cross, S., Li, X., & Huang, W. (1999). Parent-youth concordance regarding violence exposure: Relationship to youth psychosocial functioning. *Journal of Adolescent Health, 25*, 396-406.

Hu, L., & Bentler, P. M. (1999). Cutoff criteria for fit indexes in covariance structure analysis: Conventional criteria versus new alternatives. *Structural Equation Modeling, 6*, 1-55.

Huizinga, D., & Jakob-Chien, C. (1998). The contemporaneous co-occurence of serious and violent juvenile offending and other problem behaviors. In R. Loeber, & D. F. Farrington (Eds.), *Serious and violent juvenile offenders: Risk factors and successful interventions*. (pp. 47-67). Thousand Oaks, CA: Sage Publications.

Huston, A. C., McLoyd, V. C., & Coll, C. G. (1994). Children and poverty: Issues in contemporary research. *Child Development, 65,* 275-282.

Ingoldsby, E. M., & Shaw, D. S. (2002). Neighborhood contextual factors and early-starting antisocial pathways. *Clinical Child & Family Psychology Review, 5,* 21-55.

Iriondo, J. M., Albert, M. J. & Escudero, A. (2003). Structural equation models: An alternative for assessing causal relationships in threatened plant populations. *Biological Conservation, 113,* 367-377.

Jainchill, N., Hawke, J., & Messina, M. (2005). Post-treatment outcomes among adjudicated adolescent males and females in modified therapeutic community treatment. *Substance Use & Misuse, 40,* 975-996.

Jargowsky, P.A. (1997). *Poverty and place: Ghettos, barrios, and the American city.* New York: Russell Sage Foundation.

Jargowsky, P. A., & Bane, M. J. (1991). Ghetto poverty in the United States. In C. Jencks & P. E. Peterson (Eds.), *The urban underclass* (pp. 235-273). Washington, DC: Urban Institute Press.

Jennings, J. (1999). Persistent poverty in the United States: Review of theories and explanation. In L. Kushnick & J. Jennings (Eds.), *An introduction to poverty: The role of race, power, and politics* (pp. 13-38). New York: New York University Press.

Jensen, G. J., & Raymond, E. (1976). Sex differences and delinquency: An examination of popular sociological explanations. *Criminology, 13,* 427-448.

Jensen, G. F., & Brownfield, D. (1983). Parents and drugs. *Criminology, 21,* 543-554.

Jensen, G., & Thompson, K. (1990). What's class got to do with it? A further examination of power-control theory. *American Journal of Sociology, 95,* 1009-1023.

Jensen, G. F., & Rojek, D. G. (1992). *Delinquency and youth crime* (2nd ed.). Chicago: Waveland Press.

Jessor, R., Donovan, J. E., & Costa, F. M. (1991). *Beyond adolescence – Problem behavior and young adult development.* New York: Cambridge University Press.

Jessor, R., & Jessor, S. L. (1975). Adolescent development and the onset of drinking. *Journal of Studies on Alcohol, 36,* 27-51.

Jessor, R., & Jessor, S. L. (1977). *Problem behavior and psychosocial development: A longitudinal study of youth.* New York: Academic Press.

Jessor, R. (1993). Successful adolescent development among youth in high-risk settings. *American Psychologist, 48,* 127-141.

Jessor, R. (1998). *New perspectives on adolescent risk behavior.* New York: Cambridge University Press.

Johnson, B. D., Williams, T., Dei, K. A., & Sanabria, H. (1990). Drug abuse in the inner city: Impact on hard-drug users and the community. In M. Tonry & J. Q. Wilson (Eds.), *Drugs and crime* (pp. 9-67). Chicago: University of Chicago Press.

Johnston, L. D., O'Malley, P. M., & Bachman, J. G. (2001). *Monitoring the future national survey results on adolescent drug use: Overview of key findings, 2000* (NIH Publication No. 01-4923). Bethesda, MD: National Institute on Drug Abuse.

Jöreskog, K. (1971). Simultaneous factor analysis in several populations. *Psychometrika, 36,* 409-426.

Jöreskog, K., & Sörbom, D. (1983). *LISREL IV: Analysis of their structural relationships by the method of maximum likelihood.* Chicago: International Educational Services.

Jöreskog, K. G., & Sörbom, D. (1984). *LISREL 6 user's guide.* Mooresville, IN: Scientific Software, Inc.

Jöreskog, K. G., & Sörbom, D. (1996). *LISREL 8 user's reference guide.* Chicago: Scientific Software, Inc.

Juon, H. S., Doherty, E. E., & Ensminger, M. E. (2006). Childhood behavior and adult criminality: Cluster analysis in a prospective study of African Americans. *Journal of Quantitative Criminology, 22,* 193-214.

Kandel, D. B. (1978). Convergence in prospective longitudinal surveys of drug use in normal populations. In D. B. Kandel (Ed.). *Longitudinal research on drug use: Empirical findings and methodological issues* (pp. 3-38). Washington, DC: Hemisphere.

Kandel, D., Davies, M., & Karuse, D. (1986). The consequences in young adulthood of adolescent drug involvement. *Archives of General Pscychiatry, 43,* 745-754.

Kandel, D. B. (1986). Processes of peer influences in adolescence. In R. K. Silbereisen (Ed.), *Development as Action in Context* (pp. 33-52). Berlin: Springer-Verlag.

Kandel, D. B., & Andrews, K. (1987). Processes of adolescent socialization by parents and peers. *International Journal of Addictions, 22*, 319-342.

Karp, D. A., Stone, G. P., & Yoels, W. C. (1991). *Being urban: A sociology of city life.* Westport, CT: Praeger.

Kasarda, J. D. (1992). The severely distressed in economically transforming cities. In A. V. Harrell, & G. E. Peterson (Eds.), *Drugs, Crime and Social Isolation: Barriers to Urban Opportunity* (pp. 147-179). Washington, DC: The Urban Institute.

Kearns, D., & Rosenthal, D. (2001). Substance abuse in rural America. In R. M. Moore III (Ed.), *The hidden America: Social problems in rural America for the twenty-first century* (pp. 151–178). Cranbury, NJ: Associated University Press.

Keenan, K., Loeber, R., Zhang, Q., Stouthamer-Loeber, M., & Van Kammen, W. (1995). The influence of deviant peers on the development of boys' disruptive and delinquent behavior: A temporal analysis. *Development and Psychopathology, 7*, 715-726.

Kempf, K. (1993). The empirical status of Hirschi's control theory. In F. Adler & W. S. Laufer (Eds.), *New directions in criminological theory: Advances in criminological theory* (pp. 143-185). New Brunswick, NJ: Transaction Press.

Kenny, M. E., Gallagher, L. A., Alvarez-Salvat, R., & Silsby, J. (2002). Sources of support and psychological distress among academically successful inner-city youth. *Adolescence, 37(145)*, 161 – 182.

Kirby, L. D., & Fraser, M.W. (1997). Risk and resilience in childhood. In M. W. Fraser (Ed.), *Risk and resilience in childhood: An ecological perspective* (pp. 10-33). Washington, DC: National Association of Social Workers.

Kirby, D. (2001). Understanding what works and what doesn't in reducing adolescent sexual risk-taking. *Family Planning Perspectives, 33*, 276-281.

Kochanska, G., & Murray, K. T. (2000). Mother-child mutually responsive orientation and conscience development: From toddler to early school age. *Child Development, 71*, 417-431.

Kopstein, A. N., & Roth, P. T. (1990). *Drug use among racial/ethnic minorities.* Rockville, MD: National Institute on Drug Abuse.

Kornhauser, R. R. (1978). *Social sources of delinquency: An appraisal of analytic models.* Chicago: University of Chicago Press.

Kostelecky, K. L. (2005). Parental attachment, academic achievement, life events and their relationship to alcohol and drug use during adolescence. *Journal of Adolescence, 28*, 665 - 669.

Kozol, J. (1991). *Savage inequalities: Children in America's schools.* New York: Harper Perennial.

Krieger, N., Williams, D. R., Moss, N. E. (1997). Measuring social class in US public health research: Concepts, methodologies, and guidelines. *Annual Review of Public Health, 18*, 341-378.

Krohn, M. D., & Massey, J. L. (1980). Social control and delinquent behavior: An examination of the elements of the social bond. *Sociological Quarterly, 21*, 529-543.

Kumpfer, K. L., & Alvarado, R. (1998). *Effective family strengthening interventions.* Juvenile Justice Bulletin, Family Strengthening Series. Washington, DC: U.S. Department of Justice.

Laible, D. J., Carlo, G., & Rafaelli, M. (2000). The differential relations of parent and peer attachment to adolescent adjustment. *Journal of Youth and Adolescence, 29(1)*, 45–59.

Laible, D. J., & Thompson, R. A. (2002). Mother-child conflict in the toddler years: Lessons in emotion, morality, and relationships. *Child Development, 62*, 284-300.

LaGrange, R. L., & White, H. R. (1985). Age differences in delinquency: A test of theory. *Criminology, 23*, 19-45.

Landsheer, J. A., & Dijkum, C. V. (2005). Male and female delinquency trajectories from pre through middle adolescence and their continuation in late adolescence. *Adolescence, 40(160)*, 729-748.

Lanier, M. M. (1998). *Essential criminology.* Boulder, CO: Westview Press.

Larson, T. E. (1988). Employment and unemployment of young black males. In J. T. Gibbs (Ed.), *Young, black, and male in America: An endangered species* (pp. 97-128). Dover, MA: Auburn House.

Leadbeater, B. J., Blatt, S. J., & Quinlan, D. M. (1995). Gender-linked vulnerabilitiesto depressive symptoms, stress, and problem behaviors in adolescents. *Journal of Research on Adolescents, 5*, 1-29.

LeBlanc, M. (1992). Family dynamics, adolescent delinquency, and adult criminality. *Psychiatry, 55*, 336-353.

Leighninger, M. (1996). Measuring the outcomes of community-wide study circle programs. *Public Management, 78*, 39-41.

Leventhal, T. & Brooks-Gunn, J. (2000). The neighborhoods they live in: The effects of neighborhood residence upon child and adolescent outcomes. *Psychological Bulletin, 126,* 309-337.

Li, X., & Feigelman, S. (1994). Recent and intended drug trafficking among male and female urban African American early adolescents. *Pediatrics, 93(6),* 1044-1049.

Li, X., Stanton, B., Feigelman, S., Black, M., & Romer, D. (1994). Drug trafficking and drug use among urban African American early adolescents. *Journal of Early Adolescence, 14,* 491-508.

Liebow, E. (1967). *Tally's corner: A study of Negro streetcorner men.* New York: Little, Brown, & Company, Inc.

Lilly, J. R., Cullen, F. T., & Ball, R. A. (1989). *Criminological theory: Context and consequences.* Thousand Oaks, CA: Sage.

Liska, A. E., & Reed, M. D. (1985). Ties to conventional institutions and delinquency: Estimating reciprocal effects. *American Sociological Review, 50,* 547-560.

Liska, A. E., & Bellair, P. E. (1995). Racial composition and violent crime: Convergence over time. *American Journal of Sociology, 101,* 578-610.

Loeber, R., & Stouthamer-Loeber, M. (1987). Prediction. In H. C. Quay (Ed.), *Handbook of juvenile delinquency* (pp. 325-382). New York: Wiley.

Loeber, R. (1990). Development and risk factors of juvenile antisocial behavior and delinquency. *Clinical Psychology Review, 10,* 1-41.

Loeber, R., & LeBlanc, M. (1990). Toward a developmental criminology. In M. Tonry & N. Morris (Eds.), *Crime and justice: A review of research* (pp. 375-473). Chicago: University of Chicago Press.

Loeber, R., Green, S. M., Lahey, B. B., Christ, M. A., & Frick, P. J. (1992). Developmental sequences in the age of onset of disruptive child behaviors. *Journal of Child and Family Studies, 7,* 21-41.

Loeber, R., Wung, P., Keenan, K., Giroux, B., Stouthamer-Loeber, M., Van Kammen, W. B., & Maughan, B. (1993). Developmental pathways in disruptive child behavior. *Development & Psychopathology, 5,* 101-132.

Loeber, R., & Hay, D. F. (1997). Key issues in the development of aggression and violence from childhood to early adulthood. *Annual Review of Psychology, 48,* 371-410.

Loeber, R., & Stouthamer Loeber, M. (1998). Development of juvenile aggression and violence: Some common misconceptions and controversies. *American Psychologist, 53*, 242-259.

Losel, F., & Bliesener, T. (1994). Some high-risk adolescents do not develop conduct problems: A study of protective factors. *International Journal of Behavioural Development, 17,* 753-777.

Maccoby, E. E., & Martin, J. A. (1983). Socialization in the context of the family: Parent-child interaction. In P. H. Mussen, & E. M. Hetherington (Eds.), *Handbook of Child Psychology: Socialization, Personality, and Social Development* (4th ed.) (pp. 1-101). New York: Wiley.

Mancini, J. A., & Huebner, A. J. (2004). Adolescent risk behavior patterns: Effects of structured time-use, interpersonal connections, self-system characteristics, and socio-demographic influences. *Child and Adolescent Social Work Journal, 21 (6)*, 647-668.

Marcos, A. C., & Bahr, S. J. (1988). Control theory and adolescent drug use. *Youth & Society, 19*, 395-425.

Marcoulides, G., Drezner, Z., & Schumacker, R. (1998). Model specification searches in structural equation modeling using tabular search. *Structural Equation Modeling, 5*, 365-376.

Marsh, H. W., & Hocevar, D. (1985). Application of confirmatory factor analysis to the study of self-concept: First- and higher-order factor models and their invariance across groups. *Psychological Bulletin, 97*, 562-582.

Martinez, P., & Richters, J. E. (1993). The NIMH community violence project: II. *Children's distress symptoms associated with violence exposure. Psychiatry, 56*, 22-35.

Marx, K. (1990). *Capital: A critique of political economy* (Vol. 1) (B. Fowkes, Trans.). London: Penguin Books.

Marx, K. (1990). *Capital: A critique of political economy* (Vol. 2) (B. Fowkes, Trans.). London: Penguin Books.

Marx, K. (1990). *Capital: A critique of political economy* (Vol. 3) (B. Fowkes, Trans.). London: Penguin Books.

Massey, D. S., & Denton, N. A. (1993). *American apartheid: Segregation and the making of the underclass.* Cambridge, MA: Harvard University Press.

Masten, A., & Coatsworth, J. D. (1998). The development of competence in favorable and unfavorable environments: Lessons from research on successful children. *American Psychologist, 53*, 185-204.

Masten, A., Best, K., & Garmezy, N. (1990). Resilience and development: Contributions from the study of children who overcome adversity. *Development and Psychopathology, 2,* 425-444.

Matherne, M. M., & Thomas, A. (2001). Family environment as a predictor of adolescent delinquency. *Adolescence, 36,* 655-664.

Matseuda, R. L. (1982). Testing control theory and differential association: A causal modeling approach. *American Sociological Review, 47,* 489-504.

Matsueda, R. L., & Anderson, K. (1998). The dynamics of delinquent peers and delinquent behavior. *Criminology, 36,* 269-299.

Maxon, C. L., & Klein, M. W. (1997). *Responding to troubled youth.* New York: Oxford University Press.

McBride, C. K., Paikoff, R. L., & Holmbeck, G. N. (2003). Individual and familial influences on the onset of sexual intercourse among urban, African American adolescents. *Journal of Consulting and Clinical Psychology, 71,* 159-167.

McCarthy, P., Christoffel, K., Dungy, C., Gillman, M., Rivara, F., & Takayama, J. (2000). Race/Ethnicity, gender, socioeconomic status-research exploring their effects on child health: A subject review. *Pediatrics, 105,* 1349-1351.

McGee, L., & Newcomb, M. (1992). General deviance syndrome: Expanded hierarchical evaluation at four ages from early adolescence to adulthood. *Journal of Consulting and Clinical Psychology, 60,* 766-777.

McKenry, P. C., Everett, J. E., Ramseur, H. P., & Carter, C. J. (1989). Research on black adolescents: A legacy of cultural bias. *Journal of Adolescent Research, 4,* 254-264.McLaughlin, M. W., Irby, M. A., & Longman, J. (1994). *Urban sanctuaries: Neighborhood organizations in the lives and futures of inner city youth.* San Francisco: Jossey Bass.

McLeod, J., & Shanahan, M. (1993). Poverty, parenting, and children's mental health. *American Sociological Review, 58,* 351-366.

McNeil, E. B. (1969). *Human socialization.* Belmont, CA: Brooks/Cole.

McNulty, T. L., & Bellair, P. E. (2003). Explaining racial and ethnic differences in serious adolescent violent behavior. *Criminology, 41 (3),* 709-748.

Merton, R. K. (1957). *Social theory and social structure.* New York: Free Press of Glencoe.

Messner, S. F., & Golden, R. M. (1992). Racial inequality and homicide rates: An assessment of alternative theoretical explanations. *Criminology, 30*, 421-447.

Miller, P. H. (1989). Theories of adolescent development. In J. Worell & F. Danner (Eds.), *The adolescent as decision-maker* (pp. 13-46). San Diego, CA: Academic Press.

Miller, G. E., Brehm, K. E., & Whitehouse, S. (1998). Reconceptualizing school-based prevention for antisocial behavior within a resiliency framework. *School Psychology Review, 27*, 364-380.

Millstein, S., & Moscicki, A. (1995). Sexually-transmitted disease in female adolescents: Effects of psychosocial factors and high risk behaviors. *Journal of Adolescent Health, 17*, 83-90.

Moffitt, T. E., Caspi, A., Rutter, M., & Silva, P.A. (2001). Sex differences in antisocial behaviour. Cambridge, UK: Cambridge University Press.

Morash, M. (1987). Gender, peer group experiences, and seriousness of delinquency. *Journal of Research on Crime and Delinquency, 23*, 43-67.

Morris, A. (1987). *Women, crime and criminal justice*. New York: Basil Blackwell.

Morton T. L. & Ewald, L. S. (1987). Family-based interventions for crime and delinquency. In E. K. Morris & C. J. Braukmann (Eds.), *Behavioural Approaches to Crime and Delinquency: A Handbook of Application, Research and Concepts* (pp. 271-297). New York: Plenum.

Moynihan, D. P. (1965). *The Negro family: The case for national action*. Washington, DC: U.S. Department of Labor.

Mrazek, P. J., & Haggerty, R .J. (1994). *Reducing risks for mental disorders: Frontiers for preventive intervention research*. Washington, DC: U. S. National Academy Press.

Mulaik, S. (1987). Toward a conception of causality applicable to experimentation and causal modeling. *Child Development, 58*, 18-32.

Muthén, L., & Muthén, B. (2001). *Mplus user's guide* (2nd ed.). Los Angeles: Muthén & Muthén.

Muthén, L., & Muthén, B. (2002). How to use a Monte Carlo study to decide on sample size and determine power. *Structural Equation Modeling, 9*, 599-620.

Muthen, B., & Satorra, A. (1995). Complex sample data in structural equation modeling. In P. Marsden (Ed.), *Sociological Methodology* (pp. 216-316). Hillsdale, NJ: Erlbaum.

Myers, H. F., & Taylor, S. (1998). Family contributions to risk and resilience in African American children. *Journal of Comparative Family Studies, 29,* 215-229.

Naffine, N. (1989). Toward justice for girls. *Women and Criminal Justice, 1,* 3-19.National Center for Educational Statistics (2000). *Trends in academic progress. Three decades of student performance* (Report No. NCES 2000469). Washington, DC: U. S. Department of Education, Office of Educational Research and Improvement.

National Center for Health Statistics. (2000). *Vital statistics, United States, 1998* (Table III, p. 3, 106). Hyattsville, MD: National Center for Health Statistics.

Newcomb, M., & Felix-Ortiz, M. (1992). Multiple protective and risk factors for drug use and abuse: Cross-section and prospective findings. *Journal of Personality and Social Psychology, 63,* 280-296.

Newcomb, M. D., Maddahian, E., & Bentler, P. M. (1986). Risk factors for drug use among adolescents: Concurrent and longitudinal analyses. *American Journal of Public Health, 76,* 714-726.

Nichols, T. R., Graber, J. A., Brooks-Gunn, J., & Botvin, G. J. (2006). Sex differences in overt aggression and delinquency among urban minority middle school students. *Applied Development Psychology, 27,* 78-91.

Nurco, D. N., Balter, M. B., & Kinlock, T. W. (1994). Vulnerability to narcotic addiction: Preliminary findings. *Journal of Drug Issues, 24,* 292-313.

Nurco, D. N., Hanlon, T. E., O'Grady, K. E., & Kinlock, T. W. (1997a). The association of early risk factors to opiate addiction and psychological adjustment. *Criminal Behavior and Mental Health, 7,* 213-228.

Nurco, D. N., Hanlon, T. E., O'Grady, K. E., & Kinlock, T. W. (1997b). The early emergence of narcotic addict types. *American Journal of Drug and Alcohol Abuse, 23,* 523-542.

Nye, F. I. (1958). *Family relationships and delinquent behavior.* Oxford, England: Wiley.

O'Donnell, L., O'Donnell, C., & Stueve, A. (2001). Early sexual initiation and subsequent sex-related risks among urban minority youth: The reach for health study. *Family Planning Perspectives, 33*, 268-275.

O'Donnell, D. A., Schwab-Stone, M. E., & Muyeed, A. Z. (2002). Multidimensional resilience in urban children exposed to community violence. *Child Development, 73*, 1265-1282.

Office of Juvenile Justice and Delinquency Prevention (2000). *Co-occurrence of delinquency and other delinquency problem behaviors.* Washington, DC: U.S. Department of Justice.

Okundaye, J. N. (2004). Drug trafficking and urban African American youth: Risk factors for PTSD. *Child and Adolescent Social Work Journal, 21(3)*, 285-302.

O'Leary, V. E. (1998). Strength in the face of adversity: Individual and social thriving. *The Journal of Social Issues, 54*, 425-446.

Olsson, U., Foss, T., Troye, S., & Howell, R. (2002). The performance of ML, GLS, and WLS estimation in structural equation modeling under conditions of misspecifications and nonnormality. *Structural Equation Modeling, 7*, 555-595.

Orr, D., Beiter, M., & Ingersoll, G. (1991). Premature sexual activity as an indicator of psychosocial risk. *Pediatrics, 87*, 141-147.

Osofsky, J. D., Wewers, S., Hann, D. M., & Fick, A. C. (1993). Chronic community violence: What is happening to our children. *Psychiatry: Interpersonal & Biological Processes, 56*, 36-45.

Pabon, E. (1998). Hispanic adolescent delinquency and the family. A discussion of sociocultural influences. *Adolescence, 33*, 941-956.

Pallant, J. (2001). *SPSS survival manual.* Buckingham, PA: Open University Press.

Pardini, D. A., Loeber, R., & Stouthamer-Loeber, M. (2005). Developmental shifts in parent and peer influences on boys' beliefs about delinquent behavior. *Journal of Research on Adolescence, 15 (3)*, 299-323.

Parker, R. N. (1989). Poverty, subculture of violence, and type of homicide. *Social Forces, 67*, 3-1007.

Parker, J. S., & Benson (2004). Parent-Adolescent relations and adolescent functioning: Self-esteem, substance abuse, and delinquency. *Adolescence*, 39, 519-530.

Paschall, M. J., Ringwalt, C. L., & Flewelling, R. L. (2003). Effects of parenting, father absence, and affiliation with delinquent peers on delinquent behavior among African American male adolescents. *Adolescence, 38*, 15-34.

Patterson, G .R. (1982). Coercive family process. Eugene, OR: Castalia.

Patterson, G. R., Capaldi, D., & Bank, L. (1989a). An early starter model for predicting delinquency. In D. J. Pepler, & K. H. Rubin (Eds.), *The development and treatment of childhood aggression* (pp. 42-77). Hillsdale, NJ: Erlbaum.

Patterson, G. R., DeBaryshe, E. D., & Ramsey, E. (1989b). A developmental perspective on antisocial behavior. *American Psychologist, 44,* 329-335.

Patterson, G. R., Dishion, T. J., & Yoeger, K. (2000). Adolescent growth in new forms of problem behavior: Macro-and micro-peer dynamics. *Prevention Science, 11*, 3-13.

Perez-Smith, A. M., Albus, K. E., & Weist, M. D. (2001). Exposure to violence and neighborhood affiliation among inner-city youth. *Journal of Clinical Child Psychology, 30,* 464-472.

Peters, M. F. (1997). Parenting of young children in Black families. In H. P. McAdoo (Ed.), *Black families* (pp. 167-182). Thousand Oaks, CA: Sage.

Peterson, G. E., & Harrell, A. V. (1992). Introduction: Inner-city isolation and opportunity. In A. V. Harrell & G. E. Peterson (Eds.), *Drugs, Crime, and Social Isolation, Barriers to Urban Opportunity* (pp. 1-26). Washington, DC: Urban Institute Press.

Pickrel, S. G., Hall, J. A., & Cunningham, P. B. (1997). Interventions for adolescents who abuse substances. In S. W. Henggeler & A. B. Santos (Eds.), *Innovative approaches for "difficult-to-treat" populations* (pp. 99-116). Washington, DC: American Psychiatric Press.

Piquero, N. L., Gover, A. R., MacDonald, J. M., & Piquero, A. R. (2005). The influence of delinquent peers on delinquency: Does gender matter? *Youth & Society, 36 (3),* 251-275.

Piven, F. F., & Cloward, R. (1993). *Regulating the poor: The functions of public welfare.* New York: Vintage Books.

Quay, H. (1987). *Handbook of juvenile delinquency.* New York: Wiley.Rankin, J. H., & Kern, R. (1994). Parental attachments and delinquency. *Criminology, 32*, 495-515.

Rankin, B. H., & Quane, J. M. (2002). Social contexts and urban adolescent outcomes: The interrelated effects of neighborhoods, families, and peers on African American youth. *Social Problems, 49*, 79-100.

Rankin, J. H., & Wells, L. E. (1990). The effect of parental attachments and direct controls on delinquency. *Journal of Research in Crime & Delinquency, 27*, 140-166.

Ranney, D. C. (1999). Class, race, gender, and poverty: A critique of some contemporary theories. In L. Kushnick & J. Jennings (Eds.), *A new introduction to poverty: The role of race, power, and politics* (pp. 39-56). New York: New York University Press.

Reed, R. J. (1988). Education and achievement of young Black males. In J. T. Gibbs (Ed.), *Young, Black, and male in America* (pp. 50-96). Dover, MA: Auburn House.

Reese, L. E. (2001). A qualitative investigation of perceptions of violence risk factors in low-income African American children. *Journal of Clinical Psychology, 30*, 161-172.

Resnick, M., & Blum, R. (1994). The association of consensual sexual intercourse during childhood with adolescent health risk behaviors. *Pediatrics, 94*, 907-913.

Resnick, M. D., Bearman, P. S., Blum, R. W., Bauman, K E., Harris, K M., Jones, J., Tabor, J., Beuhring, T., Sieving, R. E., Shew, M., Ireland, M., Bearinger, L. H., & Udry, J. R. (1997). Protecting adolescents from harm: Findings from the National Longitudinal Study on Adolescent Health. *Journal of the American Medical Association, 278*, 823-832.

Retherford, R. D., & Choe, M. K. (1993). *Statistical models for causal analysis.* New York: John Wiley & Sons.

Reyes, O., Gillock, K.L., Kobus, K., & Sanchez, B. (2000). A longitudinal examination of the transition into senior high school from urban, low-income status, and predominately minority backgrounds. *American Journal of Community Psychology, 28*, 519-544.

Rheingold, H. L. (1969). The social and socializing infant. In David A. Goslin (Ed.), *Handbook of Socialization Theory and Research* (pp. 779-790). Chicago: Rand McNally.

Rhodes, J. E., & Fischer, K. (1993). Spanning the gender gap: Gender differences in delinquency among inner-city adolescents. *Adolescence, 28*, 879-887.

Richman, J. M., & Bowen, G. L. (1997). School failure an ecological-interactional developmental perspective. In M. W. Fraser (Ed.), *Risk and resilience in childhood: An ecological perspective* (pp. 95-116). Washington, DC: NASW Press.

Riley, D. B., Greif, G. L., Caplan, D. L., & MacAulay, H. K. (2004). Common themes and treatment approaches in working with families of runaway youths. *The American Journal of Family Therapy, 32*, 139-153.

Robbers, M. L. P. (1999). *An interdisciplinary examination of juvenile delinquency.* Unpublished doctoral dissertation, American University, Washington, DC.

Rodney, H. E., Tachia, H. R., & Rodney, L. W. (1999). The home environment and delinquency: A study of African American adolescents. Families in society. *Journal of Contemporary Human Services, 80*, 551-559.

Rosenbaum, J. L. (1987). Social control, gender, and delinquency: An analysis of drug, property and violent offenders. *Justice Quarterly, 4*, 117-132.

Rosenbaum, J. L. (1989). Family dysfunction and female delinquency. *Crime & Delinquency, 35*, 31-44.

Rosenblum, A., Magura, S., Fong, C., Cleland, C., Norwood, C., Casella, D., Truell, J., & Curry, P. (2005). Substance use among young adolescents in HIV-affected families: Resiliency, peer deviance, and family functioning. *Substance Use & Misuse, 40*, 581-603.

Rutter, M. (1978). Family, area, and school influences in the genesis of conduct disorders. In L.A. Hersov & D. Schaffer (Eds.) *Aggression and anti-social behaviour in childhood and adolescence* (pp. 95-114). Oxford, England: Pergamon Press.

Rutter, M. (1980). *Changing youths in a changing society: Patterns of adolescent development and disorder.* Cambridge, MA: Harvard University Press.

Rutter, M., & Garmezy, M. (1983). Developmental psychopathology. In P. H. Mussen (Ed.), *Handbook of child psychology* (4th ed.). New York: Wiley.

Rutter, M. (1987). Psychosocial resilience and protective mechanisms. *American Journal of Orthopsychiatry, 57*, 316-331.

Rutter, M. (1990). Psychological resilience and protective mechanisms. In J. Rolf, A. Masten, D. Cicchetti, K. Nuechterlein, & S. Weintraub (Eds.), *Risk and protective factors in the development of psychopathology* (pp. 181-214). New York: Cambridge University Press.

Rutter, M. (1993). Resilience: Some conceptual considerations. *Journal of Adolescent Health, 14,* 626-631.

Sampson, R. J., & Laub, J. H. (1995). *Crime in the making: Pathways and turning points through life.* Cambridge, MA: Harvard University Press.

Sampson, R. J. & Laub, J. H. (1994). Urban poverty and the family context of delinquency: A new look at structure and process in a classic study. *Child Development, 65,* 523-540.

Sampson, R. J., & Raudenbush, S. (1999). Systematic social observation of public spaces: A new look at disorder in urban neighborhoods. *American Journal of Sociology 105*, 603-651.

Sarigiani, P. A., Ryan, L., & Petersen, A.C. (1999). Prevention of high-risk behaviors in adolescent women. *Society for Adolescent Medicine, 25*, 109-119.

Schaefer, R. T., & Lamm, R. P. (1998). *Sociology.* New York: McGraw Hill.

Schwab-Stone, M. E., Ayers, T. S., Kasprow, W., Voyce, C., Barone, C., Shriver, T., & Weissberg, R. (1995). No safe haven: A study of violence exposure in an urban community. *Journal of the American Academy of Child and Adolescent Psychiatry, 34,* 1343-1352.

Self-Brown, S., LeBlanc, M., & Kelley, M. L. (2004). Effects of violence exposure and daily stressors on psychological outcomes in urban adolescents. *Journal of Traumatic Stress, 17(6),* 519-527.

Seydlitz, R. (1993). Complexity in the relationships among direct and indirect parental controls and delinquency. *Youth & Society, 24,* 243-276.

Shaffer, J. W., Nurco, D. N., & Kinlock, T. W. (1984). A new classification of narcotic addicts based on type and extent of criminal activity. *Comprehensive Psychiatry, 25,* 315-328.

Shapiro, T. M. (2004). *The hidden cost of being African American: How wealth perpetuates inequality.* New York: Oxford University Press.

Shaw, C., & McKay, H. (1931). *Report on the causes of crime* (vol. 2). Washington, DC: U. S. Government Printing Office.

Shaw, S. R., & Braden, J. P. (1990). Race and gender bias in the administration of corporal punishment. *School Psychology Review, 19*, 378-383.

Shoemaker, D. J. (1984). Theories of delinquency: An examination of explanations of delinquent behavior. New York: Oxford University Press.

Sickmund, M. (2000). *Offenders in juvenile court, 1997*. Washington, DC: Office of Juvenile Justice and Delinquency Prevention.

Siegel, L. J., & Senna, J. J. (1991). *Juvenile delinquency: Theory, practice and law* (4th ed.). St. Paul, MN: West Publishing.

Sieving, R. E., Maruyama, G., Williams, C. L., & Perry, C. L., (2000). Pathways to adolescent alcohol use: Potential mechanisms of parent influence. *Journal of Research on Adolescence, 10(4)*, 489-514.

Simons, R. L., Simons, L.G., & Wallace, L.E. (2004). Families, delinquency, and crime: Linking society's most basic institution to antisocial behavior. Roxbury Publishing Company, Los Angeles, CA.

Skogan, W. G. (1990). *Disorder and decline: Crime and the spiral of decay in American neighborhoods*. New York: The Free Press.

Smetana, J. G., Crean, H. F., & Daddis, C. (2002). Family processes and problem behaviors in middle-class African American adolescents. *Journal of Research on Adolescence, 12(2)*, 275-304.

Smith, C. A., & Stern, S. B. (1997). Delinquency and antisocial behavior: A review of family processes and intervention research. *Social Service Review, 71*, 382-420.

Snyder, H. N. (2005). *Juvenile Arrests 2003*. Juvenile Justice Bulletin. Washington, D.C.: Department of Justice, Office of Juvenile Justice and Delinquency Prevention.

Snyder, H. N., & Sickmund, M. (1999). *Juvenile offenders and victims: 1999 update* (Report No. NCJ 178257). Washington, DC: U. S. Department of Justice, Office of Juvenile and Delinquency Prevention.

Somers, C. L., & Gizzi, T. J. (2001). Predicting adolescents' risky behaviors: The influence of future orientation, school involvement, and school attachment. *Adolescent and Community Health, 2(1)*, 3-11.

Sondheimer, D. L., (2001). Young female offenders: Increasingly visible yet poorly understood. *Gender Issues, 19*, 79-90.

Sowder, B. J., & Burt, M. R. (1980). *Children of heroin addicts: An assessment of health, learning, behavioral, and adjustment problems.* New York: Praeger Publishers.

Speckart, G., & Anglin, M. D. (1986). Narcotics use and crime: An overview of recent research advances. *Contemporary Drug Problems, 13,* 741-770.

Stack, C. (1974). *All our kin: Strategies for survival in a black community.* New York: Harper & Row.

Stack, S. (1982). Social structure and Swedish crime rates. *Criminology, 20,* 499-513.

Stanton, B., Xiaoming, L., Black, M., Ricardo, I., Galbraith, J., Feigelman, S., & Kaljee, L. (1996). Longitudinal stability and predictability of sexual perceptions, intensions, and behaviors among early adolescent African-Americans. *Journal of Adolescent Health, 18,* 10-19.

Stanton, B., Xiaoming, L., Pack, R., Cottrell, L., Harris, C., & Burns, J.M. (2002). Longitudinal influence of perceptions of peer and parental factors on African American adolescent risk involvement. *Journal of Urban Health, 79,* 536-548.

StatSoft, Inc. (2004). Electronic statistics textbook. Tulsa, OK: StatSoft (www.statsoft.com).

Steffensmeier, D. J., & Steffensmeier, R. H. (1980). Trends in female delinquency: An examination of arrest, juvenile court, self-report, and field data. *Criminology, 18,* 62-85.

Steffensmeier, D., & Schwartz, J. (2002). Trends in female crime: Is crime still a man's world. In Barbara Price and Natalie Sokoloff (eds.), *The Criminal Justice System and Women: Offenders, Victims, and Workers.* New York: McGraw Hill.

Steffensmeier, D., Schwartz, J., Zhong, H., & Ackerman, J. (2005). An assessment of recent trends in girls' violence using diverse longitudinal sources: Is the gender gap closing? *Criminology, 43 (2),* 2005.

Stephen, J. P. (1985). Images of deviance and social control: A sociological history. New York: McGraw-Hill.

Stern, S. B., & Smith, C. A. (1995). Family processes and delinquency in an ecological context. *Social Service Review, 69,* 703-731.

Stevens, P., & Griffin, J. (2001). Youth high-risk behaviors: Survey and results. *Journal of Addictions & Offender Counseling, 22,* 31-47.

Stewart, E. A., & Simons, R. L. (2006). Structure and culture in African American adolescent violence: A partial test of the "Code of the Street" thesis. *Justice Quarterly, 23(1)*, 1-33.

Stoiber, K. (1997). Adolescent pregnancy and parenting. In G. Bear, K. Minke, & A. Thomas (Eds.), *Childrens needs II: Development. Problems and Alternatives* (pp. 653-666). Washington, DC: National Association of School Psychologists.

Stoiber, K., & Good, B. (1998). Risk and resilience factors linked to problem behavior among urban, culturally diverse adolescents. *School of Psychology Review, 27*, 380-398.

Stormshak, E. A., Comeau, C. A., & Shepard, S. A. (2004). The relative contribution of sibling deviance and peer deviance in the prediction of substance use across middle childhood. *Journal of Abnormal Child Psychology, 32(6)*, 635-649.

Sullivan, T. J. (1992). *Applied sociology: Research and critical thinking*. New York: Macmillan.

Sullivan, R., & Wilson, M. F. (1995). New directions for research in prevention and treatment of delinquency: A review and proposal. *Adolescence, 30*, 1-17.

Sullivan, T. N., & Farrell, A. D. (1999). Identification and impact of risk and protective factors for drug use among urban African American adolescents. *Journal of Clinical Child Psychology, 28*, 122-136.

Sutton, S. E., Cowen, E. L., Crean, H. F., & Wyman, P. A. (1999). Pathways to aggression in young, highly stressed urban children. *Child Study Journal, 29*, 49-68.

Taylor, R. L. (1991). Poverty and adolescent Black males: The subculture of disengagement. In P. B. Edelman & J. Ladner (Eds.), *Adolescence and poverty* (pp. 139-162). Washington, DC: Center for National Policy Press.

Taylor, R. B. (2000). Crime and human ecology: Social disorganization vs. social efficacy. In R. Paternoster & R. Bachman (Eds.), *Explaining criminals and crime: Essays in contemporary criminological theory*. Chicago: Roxbury Publishing.

Thaxton, S., & Agnew, R. (2004). The nonlinear effects of parental and teacher attachment on delinquency: Disentangling strain from social control explanations. *Justice Quarterly, 21(4)*, 763-791.

Thornberry, T. P., Moore M., & Christenson R. L. (1985). The effect of dropping out of high school on subsequent criminal behavior. *Criminology, 23*, 3-18.

Thornton, Y. S. (1995). *The ditchdigger's daughters, A Black family's astonishing success story.* New York: Birch Lane Press.

Thornton, T., Craft, C., Dahlberg, L., Lynch, B., & Baer, K. (2000). *Best practices of youth violence prevention: A sourcebook for community action.* Atlanta, GA: Centers for Disease Control and Prevention.

Tittle, C. R., Villemez, W. J., & Smith, D. A. (1978). The myth of social class and criminality: An empirical assessment of the empirical evidence. *American Sociological Review, 43,* 643-656.

Tittle, C. R. (1980). Labeling and crime: An empirical evaluation. In W. R. Gove (Ed.), *The labeling of deviance* (pp. 241-263). Beverly Hills: Sage.

Tittle, C. R. (1983). Social class and criminal involvement: A critique of the theoretical foundation. *Social Forces, 62,* 334-358.

Tittle, C. R., & Meier, R. F. (1990). Specifying the SES/delinquency relationship. *Criminology, 28,* 271-299.

Tittle, C. R., & Meier, R. F. (1991). Specifying the SES/delinquency relationship by social characteristics of contexts. *Journal of Research in Crime & Delinquency, 28,* 430-455.

Tolan, P., Cromwell, R., & Brusswell, M. (1986). Family therapy with delinquents: A critical review of the literature. *Family Process, 25,* 619-649.

Tolan, P. H., Gorman-Smith, D., Henry, D. B. (2003). The developmental ecology of urban males' youth violence. *Developmental Psychology, 39(2),* 274-291.

Tomori, M., Zalar, B., Plesnicar, B. K., Ziherl, S., & Stergar, E. (2001). Smoking in relation to psychosocial risk factors in adolescents. *European Child & Adolescent Psychiatry, 10,* 143-150.

Tremblay, R. E., Phil, R.O., Vitaro, F., & Dobkin, P.L. (1994). Predicting early onset of male AB from preschool behavior. *Archives of General Psychiatry, 51,* 732-739.

U.S. Department of Health and Human Services (2001). *Youth Violence: A Report of the Surgeon General.* Rockville, MD: U.S. Department of Health and Human Services, Centers for Disease Control and Prevention, National Center for Injury Prevention and Control; Substance Abuse and Mental Health Services Administration, Center for Mental Health Services; and National Institutes of Health, National Institute of Mental Health.

Vega, W., Zimmerman, R., Warheit, G., Apospori, E., & Gil, A. (1993). Risk factors for early adolescent drug use in four ethnic & racial groups. *American Journal of Public Health, 83*, 185-189.

Vitaro, F., Brendgen, M., & Tremblay, R. E. (2000). Influence of deviant friends on delinquency: Searching for moderator variables. *Journal of Abnormal Child Psychology, 28*, 313-325.

Voelkl, K. E., Welte, J. W., & Wieczorek, W. F. (1999). Schooling and delinquency among white and African American adolescents. *Urban Education, 34*, 69-88.

Vogt, W. P. (1999). *Dictionary of statistics & methodology* (2nd ed.). Thousand Oaks, CA: Sage.

Vold, G., & Bernard, T. (1986). *Theoretical* criminology (3rd ed.) New York: Oxford University Press.

Vold, G. B., Bernard, T. J., & Snipes, J. B. (1998). *Theoretical criminology* (4th ed.). New York: Oxford University Press.

Vold, G. B., Bernard, T. J., & Snipes, J. B. (2001). *Theoretical criminology* (5th ed.). New York: Oxford University Press.

Volk, R. J., Edwards, D. W., Lewis, R. A., Sprenkle, D. H. (1989). Family systems of adolescent substance abusers. *Journal of Applied and Child Studies, 28*, 266-272.

Wadsworth, T. (2000). Labor markets, delinquency, and social control theory: An empirical assessment of the mediating process. *Social Forces, 78*, 1041-1066.

Wagner, B. M., & Compas, B. E. (1990). Gender, instrumentality, and expressivity: Moderators of the relation between stress and psychological symptoms during adolescence. *American Journal of Community Psychology, 18*, 383-406.

Wallace, J. M., Bachman J. G., O'Malley, P. M., Schulenberg, J. E., Cooper, S. M., & Johnston, L. D. (2003). Gender and ethnic differences in smoking, drinking, and illicit drug use among American 8th, 10th and 12th grade students, 1976-2000. *Addiction, 98*, 225-234.

Walters, G. D. (1992). *Foundations in criminal science*. New York: Praeger Publishers.

Warr, M., & Stafford, M.C. (1991). The influence of delinquent peers: What they think or what they do? *Criminology, 29*, 851-866.

Warr, M. (1993b). Parents, peers, and delinquency. *Social Forces, 72*, 247-264.

Warr. M. (2002). Companions in crime: The social aspects of criminal conduct. Cambridge: Cambridge University Press.

Warr, M. (2005). Making delinquent friends: Adult supervision and children's affiliations. *Criminology, 43 (1)*, 77-105.

Warren M. Q. (1983). Applications of interpersonal-maturity theory to offender populations. In W. S. Laufer & J. M. Day (Eds.), *Personality theory, moral development, and criminal behavior* (pp. 23-50). Lexington, MA: Lexington Books.

Weaver, S. R., & Prelow, H. M. (2005). A mediated-moderation model of maternal parenting style, association with deviant peers, and problem behaviors in urban African American and European American adolescents. *Journal of Child and Family Studies, 14 (3)*, 343-356.

Weber, L. R., Miracle, A., & Skehan, T. (1995). Family bonding and delinquency: Racial and ethnic influences among U.S. Youth. *Human Organization, 54*, 363-372.

Webster-Stratton, C., & Taylor, T. (2001). Nipping early risk factors in the bud: Preventing substance abuse, delinquency, and violence in adolescence through interventions targeted at young children (0 to 8 years). *Prevention Science, 2*, 165-192.

Weerman, F. M., & Smeenk, W. H. (2005). Peer similarity in delinquency for different types of friends: A comparison using two measurement methods. *Criminology, 43(2)*, 499-524.

Weiss, J. G. (1987). Social class and crime. In M. R. Gottfredson, & T. Hirschi (Eds.), *Positive Criminology*. Newbury Park, CA: Sage.

Wells, L. E., & Rankin, J. H. (1988). Direct parental controls and delinquency. *Criminology, 26*, 263-285.

Wheaton, B., Muthen, B., Alwin, D. F., & Summers, G. F. (1977). Assessing reliability and stability in patent models. In D. R. Heise (Ed.), *Sociological methodology* (pp. 84-136). San Francisco: Jossey-Bass.

Wiatrowski, M. D., Griswold, D. B., & Roberts, M. K. (1981). Social control theory and delinquency. *American Sociological Review, 46*, 525-541.

Williams, T. M., & Kornblum, W. (1985). *Growing up poor*. Lexington, MA: Lexington Books.

Willoughby, T., Chalmers, H., & Busseri, M. A. (2004). Where is the syndrome? Examining co-occurrence among multiple problem behaviors in adolescence. *Journal of Consulting and Clinical Psychology, 72(6)*, 1022-1037.

Wilson, W. J. (1980). *The declining significance of race*. Chicago, IL: University of Chicago Press.

Wilson, W. J. (1987). *The truly disadvantaged: The inner city, the underclass, and public policy.* Chicago, IL: University of Chicago Press.

Wilson, W. J. (1996). *When work disappears: The world of the new urban poor.* New York: Vintage Books.

Wilson, W. J. (1999). *The bridge over the racial divide: Rising inequality and coalition politics.* Berkeley, CA: University of California Press.

Wright, E. B. R., Caspi, A., Moffitt, T. E., Miech, R. A., & Silva, P. A. (1999). Reconsidering the relationship between SES and delinquency: Causation but not correlation. *Criminology, 37,* 175-194.

Wright, J. P., & Cullen, F.T. (2001). Parental efficacy and delinquent behavior: Do control and support matter? *Criminology, 39(3),* 677-705.

Yanovitzky, I. (2005). Sensation seeking and adolescent drug use: The mediating role of association with deviant peers and pro-drug discussions. *Health Communication, 17(1),* 67-89.

Yearwood, E. L. (2002). Is there a culture of youth violence? *Culture Bound, 15,* 35-36.

Youniss, J., & Smollar, J. (1985). *Adolescent relations with mothers, fathers and friends.* Chicago: University of Chicago Press.

Zahn-Waxler, C. (1993). Warriors and worriers: Gender and psychopathology. *Development and Psychopathology, 5,* 79-90.

Index

A

African American youth, 3, 6, 19, 22, 24, 26, 28, 29, 32, 34, 45, 52, 92, 119, 123, 129, 132, 139, 140, 148, 182, 195, 196
Age Considerations, 128
ATOD, 4, 55, 62, 63, 66, 155

B

Baltimore City, 32, 51, 129, 146
Bellair & Roscigno, 2, 7, 14, 16, 44, 48, 86, 119, 121

C

Chesney-Lind, 4, 21, 49, 60, 107, 108, 124, 125, 126, 176
Crimes against property/person, 63, 65, 66, 113, 114, 157
Crimes of violence, 63, 65, 66, 156

D

Delinquency, 1, 2, 3, 4, 5, 7, 8, 9, 10, 12, 13, 14, 15, 16, 18, 19, 20, 21, 22, 23, 25, 28, 29, 35, 36, 38, 41, 43, 44, 45, 46, 47, 48, 49, 50, 52, 53, 54, 55, 56, 59, 69, 70, 82, 83, 84, 85, 86, 87, 89, 90, 91, 92, 94, 95, 96, 103, 104, 105, 106, 107, 108, 115, 119, 120, 121, 123, 124, 125, 126, 127, 128, 129, 131,
136, 138, 147, 148, 171, 173, 175, 176, 177, 179, 180, 181, 182, 183, 184, 186, 188, 189, 190, 191, 193, 194, 195, 196, 197, 198, 199, 200, 201, 202, 203, 204, 205, 206
delinquent acts, 1, 10, 23, 24, 29, 39, 57, 61, 125
deviant peers, 11, 59, 63, 66, 69, 90, 114, 115, 123, 131, 133, 137, 166, 184, 187, 205, 206
Discussion of Models, 96

E

early childhood socialization, 7, 36
estimation method, 72
existing data, 59, 136
exogenous variable, 54

F

Fit of the Models, 93
Future Directions, 139

G

Garmezy, 22, 124, 126, 138, 181, 191, 198
Gender Considerations, 20, 49, 107, 124